When He Whispers

A Book of Spiritual Reflections

MARY-ELLEN ZIOLA

ISBN 978-1-64299-069-0 (paperback)
ISBN 978-1-64299-070-6 (digital)

Christian Faith Publishing, Inc.
832 Park Avenue
Meadville, PA 16335
www.christianfaithpublishing.com

Printed in the United States of America

Contents

Faith

Daily Struggles

Beauty in Nature

Relationships

Christmas and Easter

Lest We Forget

Introspection

Family and Friends

Answered Prayers

Pets

Mercy

Mercy is my favourite word.
It means so many things.
We use it to express surprise,
and always reap what it brings.
What does mercy give to one?
The possibilities are endless.
It gives hope and peace and most of all,
it gives us all forgiveness.
Forgiveness is that special gift.
It allows us to start anew.
The most uplifting and rewarding words are
I FORGIVE YOU!

Never Alone

Wherever we come from or wherever we go.
It is a wonderful feeling that we are never alone.
Have a conversation or just give Him thanks.
He can't wait to hear the sound of our voice.
The sound of it brings Him such great joy.
He is so full of a deep and complete, love for us
He gives us everything we need and more.
He will walk with us to the ends of the earth.
He will calm our spirit and gentle our nerves.
He wraps us in His warm embrace.
He smoothes our brow with His gentle touch.
We are His children.
His love is everlasting.

Prayer of Thanks

My Heavenly Father, I thank You for the gifts You so generously bestow on me daily. Help me to always recognize their worth and to remember to thank You for them. Give me this day to try my best and all the tomorrows, to improve upon them. Help me to live my life with You always first and everything else will follow. Guide me in my daily life and make me always hunger for Your word. Amen.

Wish

I wish that I could snap my fingers and take all your pain away.
I wish that I could make it, so you would be healthy and okay.
It's such a helpless feeling to hear the distress come in your voice.
With your disease comes other ailments
of which you have no choice.
You keep yourself so healthy by exercising,
eating right, and getting your rest.
No one would ever say that you don't always give your very best.
You have learned to take everything in
stride, or as you say, God's time.
You are patient with life's ups and downs,
no mountain you can't climb.
Everything has a time and happens at its own pace.
Know He is watching over you and holding you in His embrace.

My Gift

I have been given many gifts from God, but one is fairly new.
He gave me the gift of writing and I want to share it with you.
Words and ideas come into my head and struggle to get free.
That's when I grab a pen and write them down, you see.
His gift to me flows quite freely, and the
piece is finished before I know it.
I really get quite excited and I just can't wait to show it.
I am still amazed at what comes out and that it comes from me.
I will always try to share my gift as it comes from God, you see.
He opens my eyes wider to take in the beauty around.
When I begin to write my thoughts, I barely hear a sound.
He fills my world with wonder. It's nature at its finest.
I will thank Him daily in my prayers for His continued kindness.

He Hears You

God is great. God is good.
He listens and He understood.
He knows our hopes and He knows our fears.
Never stop praying.
Your every word He hears.

My Litany to the Lord

Father of the Most High, thank You for my life.
Father of the highest heaven, thank You for my life.
Father of the whole universe, thank You for my life.
Father, creator of all things, thank You for my life.
Father, who is full of love and mercy, thank You for my life.
Father, whom I talk to daily, thank You for my life.
Father, who is always there for me, I love You.
Father, who listens to all my prayers, I love You.
Father, who answers me in His good time, I love You.
Father, who is protector of all, bless You.
Father, who gives us all hope, bless You.
Father, who is waiting for us all in heaven, bless You.
Father, who chose unblemished Mary as the Virgin Mother, Amen.
Father, who gave us His Son, Amen.
Father, who has given all judgement to Jesus, Amen.
Father, who loves us all no matter what, Amen.

Let us pray.
Lord, have mercy on us.
Christ, please hear us.
Lord, who is hope for the world, Alleluia!
Amen.

The Book of Revelations

Dedication
Emanation
Exhortation
Expectation
Exploitation
Fixation
Great Expectation
Jubilation
Limitation
Loving Nation
Notation
Ovation
Petition
Quotation
Realization
Reputation
Sensation
Tribulation
Vexation
Visitation
Visualization
United Nation

You're Always Listening

I want to take the time to say thank You.
You are always there for me.
You listen to everything that I have to say.
And You know we don't always agree.
But that doesn't matter to You.
You listen and love me even more.
You know when I need time to think.
And You know when I can open the door.
I love You more than I can understand.
But that's what I find so amazing.
You tell me exactly what I need to know.
I just need to listen to the phrasing.
When I focus on Your Word,
A calmness settles in.
It becomes so apparent.
You can hear the drop of a pin.
A new day dawns and I smile to myself.
It wasn't as bad as I thought.
It was such a waste of time.
And precious time is all we've got.
You try to tell me not to waste time on worry.
You have it covered with Your grace.
All I need to remember to do is
focus on Your Face.

In the Quiet

In the quiet of time, in a moment of thought,
do you think about Me as I think about you?
In that passage of space where you meet your reflection,
do you take time to look for Me in the fresh morning dew?
I created this beauty for you to use and enjoy.
Some will drink in its beauty with their eyes.
Others will capture the beauty with camera or paint.
However, you receive it. The gift never dies.
I am with you through every moment of your life.
Come, follow Me and I will enhance your living.
The love I have for you goes beyond your understanding.
It is so full and complete and mercifully forgiving.
I will be waiting for you whenever you're ready.
I will wait until the end of time. It is never too late.
You are so very important to Me.
Trust in My truth and it will open the gate.

What Wouldn't He Do for Us

He wouldn't hold anything we have ever done against us.
He would never be angry with us.
He would never leave us alone.
He would never ignore our pleas.
He will always love us beyond our own imagination.
He will always encourage us.
He will always listen to us.
He will always be with each one if us.
He will wait for us until the last possible moment.
It is never too late. There will always be enough time.
With Him, all things are made possible.
He is, was, and will always be.
He is the One in Three and the Lamb.
He is the One. The great, I Am.

A Perfect Place

There is a perfect place for each of us,
a place where we feel peace.
If we listen to His voice,
we will hear it in the breeze.
It's in the wind that blows through the field
and in the rain that beats on the roof.
He is everywhere, waiting for you.
Stop being so aloof.
He knows that you are afraid to listen,
because that means you'll have to act.
He says to us all, "Fear not!
With you, I have made a pact.
Here is the promise I have made to you.
It is more simple than you can imagine.
Love one another as yourself
and ask forgiveness for your sin.
When we have pure love in our hearts,
it leaves no room for hate.
Live your life with Me in your heart,
and Saint Peter will open the gate."

Love Misunderstood

He has ascended to His Father.
He did not die in vain.
He died with the sins of all of us.
He suffered immense pain.
He was placed on this earth for one reason alone,
and that was to save humanity.
Those that fulfilled what was decreed
have questioned their own sanity.
Pilate asked, "What is truth?"
And Caiaphas asked the same.
They must live with their own actions.
Can you do the same?

My Prayer of Gratitude

I have joy within my heart.
I feel all warm inside.
I think of my family and the love we all share,
and my smile, I cannot hide.
My smile encompasses more than you know.
I have so much to be thankful for.
He has given me so many gifts.
I am thankful to the core.

Renew Me

Jesus, please live deep within my heart.
I made time and room for You.
When You're with me, I feel whole,
and I know what I should do.
When I try to go it alone,
the way is dark and lonely.
Help me to always remember
that You are the One and Only.
You travelled this road that we are on.
You gave us a big head start.
You gave Your life for each one of us.
You have the most loving Heart.
We are Your children and will sometimes fail,
but that's when You love us the most.
You hold us lovingly in Your arms.
You are our Heavenly Host.
You are always encouraging us with Your love.
You help us to want to succeed.
Thank You for loving us and all our mistakes.
We will follow You wherever You lead.

A Holy Rite of Passage

As you make your Holy Confirmation,
You are completing your Baptismal Grace.
You are enriched with special strength of the Holy Spirit.
You are tightly wrapped in His embrace.
You are now a true witness of Christ,
Obliged to spread and defend His word.
You are His newly appointed disciple.
Your eyes are open. They are not blurred.
There may be times when you are unsure.
Say a prayer and look upon His face.
Take a breath and always remember
you are anointed with His Grace.

How Do We Get There?

God made us a loving people, and then came Satan.
He hated everything the Lord created.
To him, it was an infestation.
He thought he was perfect in every way.
But God knew better and cast him away.
Satan was once precious and good.
But when greed hit his soul,
then that became his food.
Greed feeds off of and never nourishes.
Good dies and evil flourishes.
If heaven is our hope of destination,
how do we get there, and what's God's expectation?
All He has ever asked of us is to love one another.
Love your neighbor as your brother.
It seems so simple, but as we all learn,
heaven is something that we have to earn.
God knows our hearts. They were made for truth.
That's why when we lie, it's ourselves that we hurt.
Evil lives in darkness, and goodness lives in light.
Goodness will soothe your brow, where evil takes a bite.
We know when we do something wrong, because we try to hide it.
Open the box of lies and take a look inside it.
There is condemnation and shame, and it
comes from our own conscience.
We know exactly what we are doing, every minute of every day.
You asked, "How do we get there?"
Follow Jesus. He is the way.

Running on Faith

Good and faithful servant, I have a job for you.
Will you take the challenge and do what I ask,
or look around and say, "Who are You talking to?"
Unfortunately, it won't be easy, but where is the reward in that?
There will be many things to complicate your journey
and times when you will be frustrated and want to turn your back.
There will be times of contentment and
joy and pride in all that you do.
Those are the times for peace and reflection.
You will need them to carry you through.
The promise that I make to you is one that is written in stone.
I promise to walk every mile with you,
and you will never be alone.

Journey on Foot

Each foot was placed in front of the other, bringing Him
closer to the greatest pain and the greatest gift He could
ever bestow on the one He loved so completely.
That one is everyone that He created.
He was nothing but love, gentleness, kindness,
and mercy, and yet He was feared.
The fear stemmed from our shame. We refused to
truly look at ourselves, so we got rid of the sweetness
and light that had asked us the question.
Do we really believe that following the truth of our Saviour,
which will give us an eternity of grace filled with a warmth
of mercy and love eternally, is not worth fighting for?
Life on earth is simply a stop gap filled with choices.
Life on earth is also very short. We know that Jesus is the
treasury of everything good and He is of light. His light is
where there is nothing but warmth, love, and a feeling of
protection. He will never leave us, but we have to choose Him.
We know that the opposite of good is evil and the opposite
of light is darkness. There is no warmth in the darkness.
Darkness has nothing to offer but an eternity of fear and a
coldness that seeps deeply into your core. So deep that you
will never be warm again. The kind of chill that brings with
it only loneliness and pain. A physical, heart wrenching,
eternal pain that will leave you in eternal anguish.
I choose The Light of the World. He made me and loves me fully.
Satan only wants you so that Jesus can't have you. He will
try to lure you any way he can. He is not invested in you
and doesn't love you. He hates you and wants to destroy you,
because you were created by God, and he hates God more.
Don't let the devil win! Don't let him in.

My Promise

My heart feels absolute joy at the sound
of the wind through the trees.
I close my eyes as the coolness of the breeze caresses my skin.
I am surrounded by my Father's creation.
It came from nothingness into incredible
brilliance at His very whim.
As I sit and contemplate my world, I am amazed
and humbled at the gifts He has given to me.
He has entrusted to me my parents, my siblings,
my husband, my relatives, and my friends.
I bow my head at the honour and trust of this
wonderful life He has made just for me.
I accept it with gratitude and a promise to take it all and
nurture it so that it will grow and multiply. I will offer
new shoots as gifts to be planted and cared for, so that
my garden will continue to bear the fruit of love and
mercy, which I offer freely to everyone that I meet.
It is gifted through a smile, a laugh, a helping
hand, or an ear just to be heard.
It is done in acceptance of God's love and mercy for me.
If my garden can grow from sharing, it also grows from accepting
simple gifts of love and caring. I pledge to grow my garden till I can
tend it no more and I accept all gifts with the love they deserve.

Whatever It Takes

When you are given a truth you already know to be true
and it comes from a stranger sitting beside you,
something happens in your heart it begins to feel quite warm.
Like the calm that happens after a thunderstorm,
Jesus finds us wherever we are and stands
with us to give us new strength.
He will do whatever He has to, and He'll go to any length
to tell us how much He loves us and what we mean to Him.
He is the tree so strong and true and we are His every limb.
Each one of us, He made unique. No two people are the same.
He knows us all by heart and He calls us all by name.
Nothing that happens is coincidence, but rather His design.
His message will find a way to get to us all in His good time.
If you keep your eyes open and your heart full of love,
you will know Him when you see Him. He fits like a glove.

A Conversation

You pray in that voice you reserve for His ears,
the very way you've said them for years.
You have had long talks and short ones too.
You have told Him everything, from old to new.
When you settle in for your private conversation,
your heart is filled with such elation.
You can tell Him anything with no need to worry.
He has all kinds of time and is in no hurry.
He loves you so deeply and cares how you feel.
He cherishes the relationship and helps you to heal.
He takes away the pain and replaces it with joy.
His love and mercy is endless and His to employ.
When life is going well, please don't stay away.
He wants to still hear about your every day.
Give Him your joys as well as your sorrows.
He wants to be a part of all your tomorrows.
He was there for your birth.
And He'll be there when you die.
He never left you for a moment.
So please don't cry.
He will catch your tears.
He recognizes each one.
You are His forever.
You shine bright like the sun.

Grow the Seed

To the Father, you said with all of your heart, "I trust in Your will."
You give to others till they have what they need.
You take all the pain and accept it as a gift.
He is your Gardener and you are His seed.
To the Father, you said with all of your heart, "I trust in Your will."
You go about your day, completing all of your tasks.
You give of yourself with new joy and contentment.
You listen in peace and do all that He asks.
To the Father, you said with all of your heart, "I trust in Your will."
He loves all of His creations, each and every single one.
How overjoyed He is when you live out His word.
It is your continued honour and glory that you show to His Son.
To the Father, you said with all of your heart, "I trust in Your will."
You grow your family in faith, love, and prayer,
then watch how if flourishes each and every day.
All things are possible in His tender loving care.
To the Father, you said with all of your heart, "I trust in Your will."
Life will go on. It is all up to Him.
It's been planned for an eternity.
His light will not dim.
Because of that trust you so fervently gave,
His gift to you is to continue to be brave.
There is a place for you in heaven.
You will see again His Son,
for you have always known, His will be done.

With Him There Is No Hunger

Jesus is the true substantial harvest.
Spring is the season of new life.
He was crucified, died, and was buried.
He rose up through the earth, and
His food will keep us from starvation.
He will nourish us forever.
His love is bountiful and
His harvest is always ready to eat.
Come to His table of life.
Come join in the feast.

Fear Not

Her love for the Father and all that He is
only strengthened her decision to
wholly and fully lay her life at His feet. She
called upon Him to take full control
and His will be done. She blessed herself,
when her prayers were finished, and
experienced such a calming peace.
Her faith in God is how she lives her life. He has
continually answered her pleas. He has continued to reveal
to her His absolute love and truth. She fears nothing,
as Her Father has full control over all things.
This child of God continues to testify to His word.
The miracles that He places before her fill her with
such awe at His infinite mercy, love, and grace.
Through her, I am strengthened and see Him more lovingly
and clearly than ever before. I give Him praise and honour
and glory and ask Him to continue to watch over us all.
Thank You to my Lord and Saviour. May we continue
to reap the rewards of Your infinite love.

His Power

You've discovered that you have an addiction.
You hold on to the pains of old.
You keep them with you safe and warm.
They germinate and grow like mould.
When You are feeling sad and weak,
they grow some more
and its light they seek.
To the surface, they come and then burst forth.
They become chains around your heart
and squeeze for all their worth.
The sadness moves in and stays for a while.
You can't seem to send it on its way.
It creeps into every crack and crevice
and even changes words that you want to say
where normally, you would be strong
and hear only what is said.
Now, you are reading between the lines
and your pain is being fed.
Things are being misunderstood.
That is how the devil works.
He watches everything unfold.
He stirs the pot and smiles and smirks.
This is what Satan does, and he has perfected it over time.
He keeps us feeling depressed and alone.
And the mold turns into slime.
But just when Satan thinks he's won,
the chains begin to weaken.
You found the strength to whisper a prayer,
and His answer shines like a beacon.
There is no darkness in the light.
Satan has lost his pull.
He can't exist with light and love,
and now your heart is full.

Serenity

The heart feels intensely the emotions of life.
Good things warm the heart. Bad things cut like a knife.
Health is something that we can't always control.
What we put in our bodies should be good for the soul.
When things don't go the way, we expect.
Then, nine times out of ten, stress is the effect.
Take some time and try to calm your spirit.
Whatever you do, don't let evil near it.
Close your eyes and say a prayer.
Wherever you are, God will be there.
He will wrap you in His warmth and protection.
His love for you is pure perfection.
Believe it, feel it, know it to be true.
The love you have for Him is a fraction of what He has for you.

His Awesome Power

We held him up to Your unfathomable power.
We left him in Your hands.
There's no better place that he could be
than in the Son of Man's.
You love us deeply with all Your might
and then love us some more.
We know that when we call or knock,
You're quick to open the door.
We come to You on bended knee.
We look upon Your face.
The love that is reflected back
is Your mercy and Your grace.

How Do I Say Thank You?

These two words can say everything.
We use them every day.
Most recently, You were barraged with prayers.
Each one of us came to You to pray.
We implored You to intercede.
We begged You to keep Jay safe.
You kept him comfortable for the waiting days
till the surgery could take place.
You guided the surgeon's every move.
The scalpel cuts were swift and precise.
They got the piece of bone they needed
to stop the bleeding and save Jay's life.
The days to follow will tell the tale.
We are waiting for him to come around.
Please continue to heal him as he sleeps,
and keep him safe and sound.
So after all that he's been through,
those two words seem so inept.
But since they are all that we can say,
we hope that You accept
our grateful thanks and our gratitude
for answering all our prayers.
We felt so helpless while we waited,
but You calmed all our fears.
You enveloped us in Your arms of mercy.
You kissed us with Your grace.
You were with us every step of the way.
We were wrapped in Your embrace.

Whispers on the Wind

I see You in the moving clouds.
I see You in the rain.
I see You in the bolt of lightning.
The thunder is Your refrain.
The wind carries the verses.
The words are Yours to share.
I heard You and I whispered back.
Did You hear my prayer?
I thanked You for the life You gave.
Faith and love, fan the flame.
The fire is Your continued presence,
to all those who give You blame.
If they would only close their eyes
and listen for Your voice.
They would know exactly what to do.
You are truly the only choice.
You see each of us as we really are.
Your hope is that we see You too.
You will love us till the very end,
but we have to come to You.
Your door is always opened wide.
You will continue to draw us near.
Speak to us in the whispers of the wind,
until we hear You loud and clear.

How Have You Been?

I sat outside on my screened in porch.
I needed the silence so I could think.
I have been busy of late and have missed our chats.
I'm no longer afloat but have begun to sink.
You give me the peace and the joy that I need.
I know You are with me all of the time.
When I am too busy, the road is harder.
When I bring You with me, the taller the
mountain, the easier the climb.
Thank You for loving me with no strings and no guilt.
It doesn't matter to You how much time has gone by.
Even when I put You way down on my list.
You wait lovingly and patiently to lift me way up high.
I have no words to express to You exactly how You make me feel.
You give me so much strength as I sit steeped in Your tranquil grace.
I know that when I talk to You, the peace I feel is complete.
When I close my eyes, it is there, that I can clearly see Your face.

Living His Word

If you teach your children about our Triune God,
and show kindness to everyone you meet.
If you help out wherever you see a need,
and put others first.
If you live your life this way, then you are His disciple.
When the Holy Spirit speaks and you listen with your heart,
when you act out of love with no expectation,
when you are happy and find peace at the end of a day,
when you follow His teachings and live your life by His word,
then you are His disciple.
He will bestow many blessings, many graces, and many gifts.
He always rewards us for living our best life.
A parent, loving and guiding their children.
A child, caring for a parent when they can
no longer care for themselves.
A couple, honouring the sanctity of their marriage.
Till death do you part are not empty words.
When life hands you troubles, then meet them head on.
There are no guarantees that our life will be easy.
In fact, the only guarantee is that it will be our life.
How we choose to live it is the freedom that He gave.
Your first gift from God is the very life you have.
Your second gift from God is His constant presence in it.
What will you Do? Will you call on your Father?
Will you talk to Him daily and ask Him for guidance?
He has all the answers to all of our questions.
He will wait for us to begin the relationship with Him.
He loves us beyond what we will ever comprehend.
His love is everlasting and will be with us till the end.
He'll wait forever, but why would you let Him?
He's the final piece to every puzzle.
He's the key that opens every door.
He will give you everything you've ever needed and more.

See the Blessings

Sadness. Exhaustion. Life's lost its fun.
I think the darkness thinks it's won.
I see the palest shade of light and
know I made it through the night.
My body feels the aches of drained emotion.
I stay in bed, cocooned with the notion
that God's love is all I will ever need.
It is the food on which I feed.
As long as I remember to give Him my all,
I know that He will never let me fall.
I may get bruised along the way.
But bruises heal and fade away.
I don't understand those who live without God.
Their life is a fake, a sham, a fraud.
He has given us everything, including His life.
He was beaten and whipped and cut with a knife.
The whip they used was a cat-of-nine-tails.
It tore His flesh and ripped out His nails.
As He pulled himself up to show them His strength,
He would do anything for us and go to any length.
We all know His truth, but don't want to make time
to show Him our love, and that is the crime.
He did all that He did for you and for me.
What will it take before we all see,
that His love and His mercy have always been free?
His path is all kindness, all love, and all light.
The other path leads deep into the night.
Get used to the darkness if this is your choice.
With Satan, he hates the sound of the Father's voice.
Satan laughs loudest when people act in the dark.

They know what they're doing is wrong, so hark!
It's not over yet! There is always hope.
The choice is yours. God will help you to cope.
This life is short and decides only one thing,
the light of Heaven or Satan's bling.
So, go in peace. It is yours to take.
Share it with others. It is yours to make.

Believe in Yourself

He made you with a big kind heart.
He gave you strong faith right from the start.
There are times when you doubt the gifts He has given you.
He smiles and wraps His loving arms around you.
You always talk to the Lord above.
He knows you can feel the warmth of His love.
You will always be one of His disciples.
Plant your seed. It will be fruitful.
Never doubt yourself, my child.
When He died, your name was filed.
It is listed with all the believers.
He wants you to pray for all the deceivers.
He knows He can trust in your love.
He is the Holy One above.
Your soul is marked and knows where to go.
When the time has come and all has been done,
don't fret. You will see Him, little one.

The Seed

Human life is a prayer. It's a gift from the Father.
Grow in love and faith and you will grow in ways
that will give you such joy and peace.
When you grow peace and love in your heart, it
will overflow with the seed that was planted.
When that seed falls on good soil and is cared
for, it will again bear much fruit.
When the fruit is consumed, it will be so sweet
and filling that you will want to share it.
Bloom where you are planted. You are the seed,
full of sweetness and quite substantial.
Love can feed the world, and the beauty of
it is that everyone has the seed.
It can grow in all types of weather conditions and every kind of soil.
If it is well cared for, it will bloom for an eternity.
Are you the gardener I've been looking for?

Your Tireless Love

Why do You love us so much?
Why do You keep giving us chances?
What have we done to deserve such mercy
when we look at those in need with uncaring glances?
You never give up on us when we give up on ourselves.
We are lazy and selfish and set in our ways.
You encourage us all to show one another love.
We become less afraid to live better days.
What's the worst thing that can happen
when you help someone in need?
It will allow you to feel good
and be proud of the deed.
To ease another person's trials
and to witness them, stand taller.
Is to help them carry a burden
and make their load a little smaller.
It doesn't take much to help make a difference.
All you need are giving hands and a kind heart.
Let's open our eyes to those around us.
We'll make a better world if we all do our part.

The Spiritual Hoarder

I have become a bit of a collector.
I like to stock up whenever I can.
I look for things that inspire me,
and now I've become a fan.
Space is getting tight and
I'm running out of room.
I didn't think I was a hoarder,
but truth be told, I'm doomed.
It is a sickness I've discovered.
I have to figure out what to do.
I have way more than I need.
May I give some spirituality to you?

Healing

The day is overcast with no leaves on the trees.
It's dull and grey and feels lonely to me.
Nature is resting until the Spring,
where new life will abound and grow wild and free.
The sun will come up and shine bright in the sky,
and newness will cover the land.
You will overcome your hurdles
and He will help you stand.
It is always darkest before a storm.
His light is on its way.
If you can weather the thunderstorms,
then everything will be okay.

The Prize

You sat with me on my sunporch.
I felt Your peace fill my soul.
I looked out past the screened in windows,
looked at the beauty and saw Your role.
You are the Master of creation
in heaven and on the earth.
You are the One True God.
You are the Miraculous New Birth.
You came so that we might live.
Your gifts and mercies know no bounds.
Oh Lord, please help us through this life.
Without You we have no grounds
to hope to make it into heaven.
It is the only real prize.
My prayer is that when I die,
I'll get to gaze into Your eyes.

Twists and Turns

He sat with me again today.
I bowed my head and began to pray.
His nearness gave me such inner peace
that all the outside noises ceased.
It let me focus on His voice.
He gave us all the gift of choice.
He has always shown us His gentle side,
His wrath is directed toward the evil tide.
His rules are so simple to follow.
When we go astray, we just feel hollow.
In order for Him to fill our souls,
we must dig down deep and fill those holes
that were made from all the emptiness we chose.
It was the road most travelled and was easy and smooth.
No hills or rocks to wreck our shoes.
There were no winding curves to manoeuvre.
It was short and straight and lead to nowhere.
It was missing something and nothing felt right.
I switched roads and looked up with fright.
The road seemed to go on and on.
There were rocks and hills to walk upon.
I noticed that the road kept rising.
It was going up higher. I was realizing
it was hard work and my lungs were burning.
As I trudged on, I was listening and learning.
His word surrounded me and gave me comfort
as I journeyed this path or trail of some sort.
I was feeling joy and peace and love.

This is given freely from the Father above.
Be brave and take the road less travelled.
It is rough, not paved, but dirty and gravelled.
It will take you longer to get where you're going.
But when you get there, your heart will be glowing
with the knowledge that He kept every word that He gave.
If you come and follow Him, then your soul will be saved.

Be the Change

My life is a prayer that will end in amen.
I will live each day as if it is the end.
I want to live my life as God intended.
Kindness and mercy, with no one offended.
I will treat each person as I want to be treated.
If we all do this, then hate will be defeated.
It doesn't cost anything, but willingness and action.
And a world that will live in peace with great satisfaction.
It starts with one person showing mercy to another.
Pay a kindness forward to a sister or a brother.
Let's witness what can happen in a world of daily kindness.
Where the lack of human goodness is no longer from our blindness.
We can see the world before us and close our eyes to the truth.
But I'd rather be the change and put down stronger roots.
Let's look at one another with soft eyes and a warm smile.
It might be the only kindness that person
has been shown in a while.
When your time has come and your prayer is at its end,
they will smile, say goodbye, and close with an amen.

The Way

The Lord said, "I Am the Way, the Truth, and the Light.
Listen to My voice and follow My path.
You are Mine. I created you from dust.
Be honest, faithful, true, and just.
I love you yesterday, today, and tomorrow.
I will share your pain and heal your sorrow.
I am here just for you.
Are you there just for Me?
We will walk the path together.
It won't be easy. You know heaven isn't free.
All that I ask of you is to be kind to one another.
Help feed the poor and give clothes to your brother.
Come to My house to find peace and rest.
I'll be sitting there beside you,
always giving you My best.
I love you!

He Raised Us Up

You did Your job and did it well.
You died and rose again.
You kept Your promise to the world.
And with us You remain.
You never really left us.
Your promise held fast and true.
You promised to walk with us forever
and live with us anew.
You sit at our Father's right hand.
You are the judge of the living and the dead.
You were crucified for us all.
And for us You were brutalized and bled.
Our thanks seems so inadequate,
as eternal life to us was Your gift.
You love us beyond what we can imagine.
With You as our captain, we will never float adrift.
We will not suffer indecision or confusion.
You give us absolutes. All we have to do is believe.
You are the only truth we need.
When we lose a loved one, there is no need to grieve.
We will see them all again
when it is our time to go.
By Your death, we were gifted eternity.
We need not fear the cock's crow.
Talk with You and walk with You.
Is that all it really takes?
Be still and listen for His voice,
and you'll make fewer mistakes.

He wants us all to succeed.
He has given us all the clues.
Read the instructions carefully.
The end result is the key to use.
It will open many doors
along the way as you walk your road,
but most importantly, remember,
to enter heaven, it is the code.

I Bow My Head in Quiet Praise

In a few short hours, Your life's true purpose will begin.
Your human self is feeling pain, fear, and sadness, while
Your divine self is knowing, obedient, kind, and loving.
Your selfless act is so incredibly pure and giving and so
full of love for us that in our pitiful humanness, we
sometimes forget, exactly, what You have given to us.
Forgive us our selfish stupidity.
Help us to remember that this life is only a very short walk
to a crossroad.
In our short time on earth, You give us free will to choose to
live our life by Your teachings or be swallowed up by worldly ways.
Your way is much harder and offers the
only reward and You walk with us
every step of the way.
The other path leads to nothingness and is easy and takes no effort.
Two choices: Eternal life or Eternal death.
Your life and death are gifts to us all.
You will always love us, but only we can choose to love You.
Thank You, Most Holy, Mighty, Immortal One.
I beg of You to always walk with me.
All my gratitude, praise, and honour to You.
Your loving child, always.

Shine

He gives us so many blessings and opportunities.
He gives us ways that we can shine.
He doesn't give us frilly and finished.
But something we can design.
We mould, shape, and create.
Herein lies the challenge.
We are doing our best work for God.
He is the one who will judge the balance.
He will never give us more than we can handle.
This is where we see how truly strong we are.
Some will give up and never see their potential.
Others will blame Him and let hate rule their heart.
Those that do their best have brought Him along the way.
If we're smart, we'll realize that we can't do it alone.
We will not succeed, however hard we try.
And our hearts will turn to stone.
He doesn't want us to fail.
That was never His intention.
He made us for love and friendship.
We are His greatest invention.
He always knows what He is doing.
He has never made a mistake.
How we decide to use His gifts
will be the life we choose to make.

Wonderful Healer

Merciful, wonderful, healing Physician,
Creator of all living things,
we praise and honour You for the blessings You give.
You are the King of Kings.
We thank You for everything You have done
where Your child Jason is concerned.
We ask for continued guidance
in all the things we've learned.
You revealed Your Majestic Glory
for all of us to see.
Please continue to watch over him
until he is healed and free.

Amen.

Butterfly

You must crawl before you walk.
You must babble before you talk.
You must be emotional before you cry.
You must spread your wings before you fly.
You have left your old cocoon behind.
Your eyes are open. You are not blind.
You are beginning a new chapter of your life.
You are still a mother, but no longer a wife.
You have a freedom to walk a new road.
It will be easier with a lighter load.
Go on now and give it a try.
Spread your wings, beautiful butterfly.

Hear Me

It hurts my heart when you won't let me speak.
I wonder if you ever hear me at all.
It hurts me when it's your protection that I seek.
And it feels like you let me fall.
I walk through my life not knowing if I matter.
I'm a balloon with a slow leak.
I am a pane of glass about to shatter.
Please listen to me when I speak.
I crave a conversation with you
where each of us shares our feelings.
We treat each other with respect.
We need to show that we can have these dealings.
The first time won't be easy as pride is a touchy thing.
But if we care enough about each other,
then we will witness what love can bring.
You make important decisions for me.
You never ask me for my input at all.
I feel like I'm living in a tomb with
no one to hear me when I call.
So don't be surprised when you call me
and I don't respond to your request.
I'm sitting alone in the darkness,
just trying to do my best.
If you truly love me, like you say you do.
Then please look me in the eye.
Let's start this relationship anew.
I don't want to say goodbye.

Please Help Me Lord

Dearest Lord Jesus,
I am struggling.
I need help to make sense of it.
I am asking You to help me find peace.
I need Your gentle and loving guidance
to use the tools You blessed me with.
You gave me great love, faith, and family.
It is hardest to use these tools when I am hurt or upset.
May I feel Your burning love in my heart and feel
the joy of Your presence daily.
Help me to remember to turn to You in all things.
That is when the struggle becomes a solvable problem
and peace can find its way to me again.
Amen.

Lost Souls

I think about those of Your children, Lord, who have no spirituality.
When events occur within their lives that they struggle with alone,
who do they turn to when they need
divine help and the day is done?
I am sad for those souls who believe that this
life is all that there will ever be.
They have missed out on years of faith, which
lends the strength that's needed.
When the loved ones of those souls are left behind,
who puts back together the pieces?
I believe that those lost souls, upon meeting
their Creator, are given the chance to
get to know their Father. They will be sad for a
moment to realize all the years they wasted,
but an immense joy will fill their hearts, when they
can thank and praise His Divine Mercy and love.
They will talk with Him about their fears for the family
they neglected to teach. God will smile and remind
the soul that their job has only just begun.
They will be taught how to pray for their loved ones
on earth and reminded that they are not alone.
The prayers of unimaginable numbers are said every
second and carry with them immeasurable worth.

What Do You Have to Say?

Most conversation falls on deaf ears.
It is sad to realize that you have nothing to say.
When you leave so much unsaid,
Where does that leave us at the end of the day?
I can't help but feel that you couldn't care less.
You want to close your eyes to anything negative
and just keep stepping over the mess.
When emotional health is continually ignored,
it will just keep rearing its ugly head.
Frustration and anger will replace all feelings,
and then it will just feel dead.
I don't want to keep feeling this way,
and I won't keep sweeping it under the rug.
Why do you refuse to discuss meaningful things
and make me feel like all I do is bug?
If you are happy with the way things are,
then you are not hearing or seeing me at all.
Our life together could be so much more.
When are you going to stop putting up a wall?
You have to be aware of the domino affect.
I hate getting nowhere fast.
The walls will come tumbling down,
and I don't want to live in the past.
Could we try to start all over again,
really try our very best
to show each other true love and respect,
and make honest communication our only quest?
It has to be all or nothing.

We both need to work hard at it all.
Pride has no place in this relationship,
because we know pride goeth before a fall.
Do we want to let it win?
And always know that our best wasn't given?
And if this is our best?
Then we haven't been livin'.
We have to be truly committed.
Just getting by is a pretty poor choice.
I refuse to believe that this is all it can be.
If I have to, I will scream until I have no more voice.

Show Me That You Were Listening

I feel like I fail when I try.
It frustrates me when I can't get my point across.
You never seem to understand what I say.
I feel at such a loss.
Why does it always sound better in my head?
When I say it out loud, it falls on deaf ears.
I want so much to be understood
my frustration turns into tears.
Am I asking too much from the one that I love?
Is it just my selfishness and pride?
The only thing I really need
is to know that you really tried.
If I bare my heart to you
and don't get any response,
then I will begin to think
that I'm not what your heart wants.
This is when I feel most fragile,
like feeling alone in a crowded room.
The quiet is almost deafening.
It's the calm before the storm.
All I ask is for a glimpse.
Show me that you are listening.
We need to work at this together,
Or it's all for naught and glistening
with tears of sadness for the loss
at what happens to people who stop trying.
I don't want to look back on us
and see only the tears from crying.

I won't give up trying. I can't.
I still believe in His plan for us.
But I am not foolish enough to believe
That it will all be no fuss, no muss.
There are times when we can't stand each other.
That's unfortunately our very human side.
We feel so betrayed and hurt
when we find out that the other has lied.
It is one of the most difficult things to come back from
in a relationship between a husband and wife.
How do we learn to love again
without the past overshadowing our life?
I don't know where we will end up,
but I can give you this, at least.
Every time the devil tries to interfere,
if we work together, we can slay the beast.

In a Blur

My mouth is dry, my eyes are blurred,
I feel like I am overheating.
My breathing quickens and I feel confused.
My sense of calm is fleeting.
It's happening again.
I'm losing control.
My thoughts go where they may.
I can't remember where I was going
or what I was about to say.
The walls feel like they're closing in.
The oxygen is thinning.
I have to get away from here.
I can't stop my head from spinning.
Please, can somebody help me?
I don't know what to do.
I can't go on like this.
Just, someone help. I don't care who.
The simplest task seems impossible.
All I want to do is go home.
I can't do anything more right now.
I just want to be alone.
Loneliness is the real problem.
I think about it and it makes me sad.
I know what I want for my future,
but the past was all I had.
I need to heal myself
before I can think about another.
I need to make peace with the past.

Not be a fighter, but a lover.
I know all of my good qualities,
but I lost sight of them for a while.
I need to focus on all the positives.
I'll rake the negatives into a big pile.
I'll strike a match and throw it in
and watch the debris catch fire.
The positive was telling the truth.
The negative was such a liar.
Burn, lies, burn.
Don't trouble me again.
You are evil and destructive,
and I'm gonna win.

Inside myself

I have conversations with myself at times.
And I school myself as well.
I promise myself not to mention something,
and then I go ahead and tell.
Why can't I listen to myself
and keep that bit inside?
But noooo, I have to let it out
and in him I confide.
It never comes out like it is in my head.
It just sounds like I'm whining.
And when the talk is over,
my stomach, feels like it's lost its lining.
The reaction I received was not what I intended.
I can't seem to get myself out of this hole.
I seem to have hurt us both
and that certainly wasn't the goal,
but God does work in mysterious ways.
Something always changes for the good.
I notice that the conversation is different.
He answered my prayers like He promised He would.

Under the Bridge

The things that have happened, we cannot change.
It is said that "it is water under the bridge."
The image that I see in my mind
is them being swept over the edge.
Of all the things that I could do,
I will not focus on the past.
I won't get very far if I always look behind me.
I want to move forward, but not too fast.
When we move too quickly, there are things that we will miss,
like the who, what, when, where, and why.
How can we keep moving forward
and not be content with just getting by?
When all of our actions are well thought out,
with discernment, kindness, and love,
we will make fewer mistakes and
reap the rewards from our loving Father above.
He is never far and only a word away.
He can't make it any easier than that.
He knows our heart and feels our pain
and waits for us to make contact.
He said that where there is devastation and heartache,
His mercy is overflowing.
If we don't seek Him out, when we are broken,
then the pain, will deepen and keep growing.
Why would we put our hearts through this?
It seems so senseless on our part.
He sees us and waits for us to call,
so He can begin to heal our heart.
Water is cleansing and always renews.
It keeps flowing as it clears.
So let the water flow under the bridge
and wash away all of our tears.

Can I?

I sit all alone in this room.
I am surrounded by four walls of silence.
They ask nothing from me and respect my need for peace.
Time goes by quickly and day turns into night.
I look and see that nothing has been accomplished.
How do I get off this road to nowhere?
I begin each day with possibilities.
But motivation is not my friend.
It stays just out of reach and taunts me.
I am ashamed by my indecision.
I am back in my place of solitude.
It's beginning to feel more like a prison.
Why do I willingly incarcerate myself?
What could be worse than how I have
allowed myself to live till now?
Am I willing to venture outside of my comfort zone?
If I don't at least try, then what does that make me?
Am I so afraid to fail?
What could possibly be so overwhelming for me?
I won't be able to answer these questions,
unless I am willing to really look inside myself.
Life has to offer more than I have asked of it or of myself.
"Help me," I whisper to the silence.
I get no audible response.
I realize that the answer lies within me.

I ask myself what it is I'm looking for.
What is it that I want to do with myself?
The answer reverberates around the room.
I'm tired of hiding and letting life happen without me in it.
Today, my life begins in earnest.
I will not be afraid.
I will try new things.
I will push myself a little every day.
I can do this.
I have to do this.
I just realized I want to do this.

You Have Seen My Flaws.

Why is love so hard?
It's one of the most wonderful emotions.
It gives joy, peace, a sense of self, and is easily
the best feeling in the entire world.
I know why it's so difficult.
It's because love must exist in the same world with pride.
Pride can be a good thing. But mostly, it's not.
Pride brings out the worst in us all.
For the sake of our pride, we find it hard to
hear the absolute truth about ourselves.
We refuse to admit to our own faults,
but have no trouble pointing them out in others.
And no one wants to think that our loved ones
see those blemishes that we have spent a considerable
amount of time, masking or ignoring altogether.
It especially hurts our pride when we discover that
our loved ones see through our facade and
have spoken our faults aloud.
We pretend that we only wanted to hear the truth.
But that is the first crack in the facade.
We hear it and immediately are affronted.
We go on the defensive and try to salvage
our pride by turning it around on the observer.
How can you possibly think that about me?
An argument ensues. You try to take the
glaring spotlight off yourself by deflecting it.
All along, you could hear the truth.

You aren't proud of yourself, but
you aren't willing to give in either.
Silence can be tranquil, but this silence
brings with it forced introspection. Ouch!
The gig is up.
Speak the truth that has been exposed.
This is your chance to come clean and heal.
Your energy no longer has to be wasted on appearances.
Truth, is the mirror to your soul.
No one can hide from their own reflection,
so you may as well take a good look and
love what you see, warts and all.
When you can truly love all the things about yourself,
then, and only then, can you truly love.
Fill your space with mirrors, so that
you never lose sight of yourself again.
You are beautiful.
You are loveable.
You are not perfect and that's quite all right.

I Cry

I cry for you when I think of your pain.
I cry for you and it falls like rain.
I cry for you when I think of where you go from here.
I cry for you and feel every tear that runs down your cheek
as you look at your life.
Up until now, you could deal with the strife.
Your strength and spirit always got you past the pain.
With God's help, you can do it again.
This situation will take all of your faith.
To the devil, give all of your wrath.
And to your God, who loves you so fiercely,
give Him your pain and He will give mercy.
Mercy to love and to forgive.
Your biggest decision is how will you live.
Take care of your heart and trust in the Father.
He will heal you and love you and bless you, no matter.
No matter what you have thought or felt or said.
He will enfold you and make sure you are fed.
Fed by His word. Nothing else matters.
Even if you feel, your world is in tatters.
He will lift you up and carry you on.
For He is love and His will be done.

Sometimes

Sometimes, I feel sad, and
Sometimes, I feel happy.
Sometimes, I feel broken,
and like some of the pieces are lost.
How can I mend if parts of me are missing?
How will I find them before it's too late?
Where do I start the search?
I have to return to the last place I saw them,
the place where I was happy and whole.
How do I get there?
It starts with forgiveness.
Forgive yourself for your weaknesses
and forgive the one that hurt you.
We can't be afraid of apologizing either.
Almost all of the time, the person that hurt
us is absolutely unaware of our pain.
When we apologize, it is from our own heart.
We have to move forward without expectation.
Ask for forgiveness and hope to receive it,
and then leave it in the past.
Every day, is a brand new day.
It's fresh with love and hope.
We are the ones that change the hope and love
into sadness, hurt, and pain.
So we are also the ones that can turn it back again.

Empty

I am unravelling, and I don't know if it will stop.
I can't cry one more tear.
When my thoughts go back to the hurtful words,
a total numbness is what I fear.
The day began with a glimpse of light.
Only to be shut out by anger and hate.
My life, as I know it, hangs by a thread.
I think that it's too late.
Too late to say "I'm sorry."
Those are just empty words.
My heart has been ripped out.
I feel so alone and it hurts.
My chest feels like my heart has shriveled.
I am overcome with a feeling of dread.
Please, God, don't let it happen.
Don't let the love be dead.
I could have sworn that You picked him out just for me,
a love I'd have for life.
But as the fights become more bitter,
you may as well cut me with a knife.
I don't know if I have the strength to keep trying,
I already feel like I'm in it alone.
I think you want it over with, but fear keeps you hanging on.
You feel you have no other choice. You are
trapped with nowhere to go.
The trap door is opened. You are no longer a prisoner.

Please, let's stop putting on a show.
You are free to go, with no judgement from me.
You deserve to be loved the way you want to be.
I don't know how to love you anymore.
Everything I try is thrown back in my face.
I am starting to feel worthless and ragged.
It's time to leave this place.
I am worthwhile and loving.
I thought you believed that too.
But how can we treat each other like this?
What else is there to do?

Yellow

Yellow is its blazing colour.
Some days, its shine is a little duller.
It warms everything that's in its path.
It soaks it like it's in a bath.
It heals ailments and brightens the mood.
Without the sun, we would have no food.
It helps all things grow healthy and strong.
It has been written about in many a song.
It has been high in the sky since the beginning of time.
It is the star of my little rhyme.

Wings

The hawk soared across the sky.
It dipped and rose on the wind.
It glided to a branch and perched.
It appeared to be waiting for the next breeze.
Here it comes!
The hawk crouched and pushed off from the tree limb.
And started all over again.

Surrounded by Beauty

The breeze carried on it a note of apple
blossom with a hint of cedar.
The colour of the sky was robin's egg blue
and the clouds looked like big
cotton balls suspended in time.
Nature prepares itself to feed all the wildlife by sprouting new buds.
The spring rain soaks into the earth as a reserve for drier times.
I walk in the fields and look at nature's beauty.
The robins run along the ground, looking for food.
A baby groundhog scampers for cover in the tall grass.
This is my home and I love it.

Blue Skies

I step outside into the warmth and light of another beautiful day.
The gentle breeze is cooling on the skin
as it kisses me on its way past.
The leaves sway on their branches and the
long grasses of the field bow down
to the majesty of His creation. All of nature
has their own way of praising Him.
Often, it is done in full sight of humanity. We are in awe of the
grandeur. It is a gift given without thought of repayment,
but for the simple pleasure of the lucky individual who
is chosen as the audience at that very moment.
I hope we all take the time to thank our Creator every chance
we get. Our very life is a gift. Use it and live it well.

The Iris

The bud was growing larger and it started to split and reveal some colour. Just a hint of yellow. It rained heavily in the night and drenched all growing things under the sky. The morning after, its full brilliance was on display for all to see. It was the most beautiful shade of yellow, tinged with deep violet. The outer edge boasted a lovely frill of white. It was Mother Nature, clothed in the most sought-after couture. All designers can only hope to achieve a fraction of the pure majesty of God's diverse and glorious universe. How does a dry old seed have the capability of producing such incredible awesomeness? How can a dry old seed produce the most riveting colours that humanity has spent a lifetime trying to recreate in their own designs ever since? Recreations are lovely, but will never achieve the living beauty of a flower growing out of the ground, tended and nurtured by the grower. Flowers are the masterpieces of nature. Nature is the masterpiece of our Creator. Thank You, God, for allowing us to experience a hint of what heaven may be like.

The Storm

It slaps at any object that it touches. Listen! The intensity can be deafening and then the thunder claps and growls like a lion with a sore tooth and lightning streaks down from the heavens. It wanes to a gentle shower, with light nervously peeking out through the clouds and waiting for the voice of discipline to shout back, "Close the curtains!" A few rumbles to make a point, and then there is more light and less raindrops. Everything is lush and new again, having been given the very thing needed to sustain it. The gentle breeze carries on it an earthy fragrance with hints of various blossom perfumes that when hit with droplets of water, share their gift. The clouds move on and leave behind a pale blue sky and a mist that hangs heavy in the air for a few minutes more.
It seems to remove all angst and confusion. Take a breath. Look around you. Can you take in all the majesty of the painting, newly created just for your very eyes?
Take it. It's yours.

Newness

A darkness glides across the light of the sky. It moves like
smoke from a fire. These are the rain clouds that are leaving
for a while, as their job is done. They came. They rained
and moved effortlessly through the sky, further and further
away. The clouds resembled giant herds of wildlife, moving
en masse to the next watering hole or feeding ground.
Water drips from the rain gutters. The mesh of the window screens
are filled with droplets of water that create little rivers that flow
down to the sill, where they pool and drip onto the grass below.
Like a baptism, the rain creates newness everywhere it falls.

Nature's Concerto

The wind whispered through the forest, sharing long ago
secrets. The trees bent towards one another to pass the whispers
along. The branches seemed to nod in understanding.
Knowledge and experience are passed from old to young. Each
learns how to sway and bow and bend in all types of situations.
Young ones with no experience are afraid that they won't get it
right, so they listen intently and practice under the tutelage of the
old masters. It is like watching an orchestra. The music begins,
and they are brought in by the conductor to play their part.
Ah yes! Another masterpiece!

Iridescent Beauty

Even in the dullness of the day, the blush of red at its throat was
as rich and bold, as if it was perched in a direct beam of light.
We sometimes attach a special person that has
passed to a beautiful creature in nature.
He was over six feet tall and carried himself with strength
and grace. He could sit for ages and watch the graceful
maneuverings and incredible speed, with which they
travelled from limb to limb and feeder to flower.
I watched at the window as he went out to
refill the hummingbird feeders.
Here was this giant of a man who had four of these
creatures darting in and around his arms and back,
trying to be patient as they awaited fresh food.
He would talk soothingly to them as he went about his task. And
as unassumingly, as he went out, he was back, sitting in his chair
at the window and watching intently the scene before him.
As the years pass, filling the feeders at the start of spring
and waiting to catch the first glimpse of these colourful tiny
beautiful creatures brings Dad to the forefront of my mind
and a smile to my heart. I talk to them as if it is Dad and he
has stopped by for a visit to let me know that he is okay.

The Sunflower

Our Mom liked to cook and bake.
She taught us all she knew.
This sunflower came from her kitchen,
and I would like to gift it to you.

You may place it wherever you like.
It brings with it lots of love.
When she sees them hanging in our homes,
know she is smiling from above.

A Fall Day

Autumn came in on a warm breeze. The leaves welcomed
it with a colourful ballet that had the wind as their dance
partner, twirling them into the air in a graceful pirouette before
descending to the earth on pointed stem. The ground was
decorated in an array of patchwork magic, from blue sky dotted
with white fluffy billowing clouds to vibrant green conifers,
filling in the spaces where branches in full leaf used to be.
What a difference a few days make. This day, the wind carried
with it a crispness that kissed apple red into my cheeks. An
added scarf with gloves made the walk quite enjoyable.
I took a right at the end of the road today and was rewarded
by the flash of dark brown wings silently gliding across
the road in front of me and into the dense woods.
Nature is so beautiful in movement.

What a Day!

Rain falls down and fiercely hits the ground.
The drops are oval, oblong, egg-shaped, and round.
It splashes back up and falls a second time.
But when they hit their target, they're as flat as a dime.

Rain falls sideways and is accompanied by wind.
You become drenched and almost feel pinned.
It drives with such a force. It makes the windows rattle.
It makes you more alert and ready to do battle.

You enter your sanctuary and can't wait to get dry.
You sit down for a moment and heave a great sigh.
You hear a drip and see the puddle on the floor.
You mop up the mess and slam the cupboard door.

Now you can take a minute to relax and have a cup of tea.
You shake your fist at the rain that's falling and ask, "Why me?"
You realize your groceries are still out in the car.
It has begun to rain even harder for your
course that seems to be par.

You come back in a second time and hope that it's the last.
The ice cream is beginning to melt and needs to be refrozen fast.
The counter is full of groceries that need to be put away.
Soon, it will be supper time. What a hell of a day.
You look at the clock and remember the
leak. Do you have any time at all?

You dial the number and hear the message,
"Sorry, we missed your call."
You leave your message and number and then turn and almost slip.
You walked right through the puddle without
falling and breaking your hip.

It was an accident waiting to happen, one
that should have come to pass.
Thank goodness you weren't carrying
anything that was made of glass.
By rights, you should have been on your
butt and cursing a blue streak.
You better get used to all this rain. It's supposed to fall for a week.

After

The wet grass slashes across my shoes, seeping beyond the cloth
and soaking everything inside. My shoes must have had a bit of
sand in them from the gravel road I walked on. I can feel grit
rubbing between my toes as I take steps down to the garden.
Oh well, they are wet now. I will continue my investigation. I
want to see if any damage was done in the wake of the storm.
All appears to be well. I see new growth. The rain moved soil
aside to show new shoots, reaching for the sun's warmth.
The droplets of water on the leaves shine like diamonds in
the sunlight. It is a beauty that is quite captivating and brings
with it a peace that allows the mind to rest in imagination.

A Season of Change

The gnarled planks of the barn wall are cast in
fingers of light from the morning sun.
The temperatures are rising, and the heavily snow
laden roof is beginning to melt at the edges. Wet
sloppy bits are falling to the ground, as chickadees and
squirrels crawl, play, and run across the barn wall.

Wildlife seems to pop out of every opening, crack, and
crevice, waking to a new day. They can sense the changes
in the air. They can smell the changes on the wind. They
are giddy with delight. You can see them frolicking across
the snow crusted surfaces of the land. They seem to chatter
excitedly with a newfound energy and lightness.

Spring brings out the best in all of us. It marks the end of a long,
cold and heavily burdened winter of layered clothing, snow
shoveling, slippery ice, hazardous driving conditions, and
long dark days.

The new season of spring brings promises of longer days,
warmer temperatures, less layers, new growth emerging from
the forest floor and struggling to push up through partially
thawed soil, and leaf bud filled branches just waiting to unfurl.

We see the changes that occur in each other too! Our
moods lighten. We are more forgiving of each other. We
walk with a livelier gait. We appear to thaw out as well.
The new growth we see happening before our
eyes fills us with a new spirit, a new hope,
and a full heart. We are happier and more content.

It is truly like a load has been lifted from our backs and has allowed us to stand up straighter and walk with more ease and confidence. We are rejuvenated and stronger, as we look ahead and see sunshine, new life, open waters, flowing streams, and sun-kissed skin. The trees will be clothed in lush green leaves. The noises of nature will fill the air with hustle and bustle. Spring cleaning will begin! It will be a different kind of busy from that of winter. Our windows will be opened wide and the breeze that blows in will carry on it the wonderful fresh scents of nature.

We will each embark on new endeavours. May we always remember to look at each other with soft eyes of love and acceptance. May we always be ready to lend a hand to those that need it. May our hearts be filled to overflowing and may God always walk with us in all the splendour He created especially for us.

Days End

I sat again on my sunporch as day turned into night.
The colours that I witnessed were such a glorious sight.
The most beautiful painting I'd ever seen
was splashed across the sky.
It's different every single night and is magnificent to the eye.
The colours went from yellow to orange, to red and then to violet.
It's times like these that I sit and wish that I could be a pilot.
To be among the brilliance of the colours of the sky.
To wish I were a bird and could flap my wings and fly.
I sat in wonder, as the colours of the painting began to fade away.
The darkness of night crept in slowly and
seemed to swallow up the day.
I heard the frogs and birds chirping as they began to settle in.
They were saying good night to all those around them,
until it is daylight again.

The Din

I walked through the rain and got soaked to the skin.
I heard a voice say, "Can you hear Me through the din?"
I closed my eyes and listened to see what I could hear,
and that's when I heard His voice. It came through loud and clear.
He said, "Even when the light is dim, a raindrop has a shine.
The earth glistens with heavens' tears made up of yours and mine.
Nothing goes to waste. You see, it is all reused again.
Our tears evaporate and are reserved in the
clouds until they fall as rain."
I opened my eyes and looked around. The
sun was nowhere to be seen,
and yet everything around me gave off a light, a reflection, a sheen.
He never lets the beauty of His creations hide from sight.
He is sunshine, He is shadow, He is love, and He is light.
He loves us even when we find it hard to love ourselves.
He gifts us with His creations, but more importantly, Himself.
He walks with us in every situation that we find ourselves in.
He loves us, even though He knows that each of us will sin.
He is a forgiving God when we can't find the strength.
He has demonstrated from the beginning
that He will go to any length.
It is impossible for us to fathom a love so pure and strong.
That's why some believe there is no God,
but that's where they are wrong.
He is the Ancient One and has existed through all time.
He has seen it all, every act of kindness and every senseless crime.
He created all in heaven and everything on the earth.
I want to know that when I die, I lived a life of worth.
If we are kind and loving and always lend a helping hand,
then we are living by His word and following His command.
So the next time you see a raindrop, try to take a closer look.
Can you see your reflection in the journey that it took?

Where Have You Been?

I've been watching for you for a while now. Where have you been?
I checked your regular haunts and the last places you were seen.
I couldn't find any sign of you, not even a little feather.
I couldn't find you anywhere and blamed it on the weather.
It must get so cold for you, as you look for a place to rest yourself.
You sit up high on a pine bough, like you were sitting upon a shelf.
I know you need protection from the elements and such.
Especially from the predators that like to hunt you so much.
So let me tell you how glad I was when I looked across the field.
There you were, strutting around with the tree line as your shield.
You ventured out into the open. My, but you were brave.
Imagine a large turkey showing itself on Christmas Day.
I never had a bad thought and absolutely no ill will.
I wanted to see if there was any food. Were
there nuts and seeds there still?
I tiptoed to the grain barrel and scooped up a full bowl.
I snuck out of the front door and didn't see a soul.
As I made my way up the road, you must have heard me coming.
The next thing that I heard was the sound
of your wings thrumming.
You flew across the driveway and then across the road.
I'm sorry if I frightened you and put you in panic mode.
I walked back to the house and hoped that you'd be back.
I went out to the porch and put the bowl back in the sack.
I sat down at the table and looked out past the yard.
I shuffled the deck I held in my hands and turned up another card.
A little later, as I talked on the phone, a movement caught my eye.
I saw you strut right past the spruce. A cocky little guy!
You headed directly to the spot where I had placed the seed.

I hoped the snow hadn't covered it up, so you could have a feed.
I stopped at the place where I had seen your
tracks and placed the little snack.
I noticed the snow had been disturbed,
and I knew you had been back.
I smiled as I turned away and looked down at the road.
I saw another set of prints right there, beside my own.
I followed them to the turnaround and as I was drawing near.
Again, I heard the flapping of wings as you flew away in fear.
It had been so long since I'd seen you last,
and now twice in the same day!
I'll continue to keep an eye out. Come on back. You know the way.

The Colours of Autumn

The hot summer nights turn into cool evenings that need a blanket
put back on the bed. The cold nights prepare the trees for glory.
You can see it in the hint of red around the edges of the green maple
leaves. Tinges of orange and yellow begin to show themselves.
The countryside takes on the look of a patchwork quilt
that Grandma has been working on. The last of the garden's
harvest has been brought in out of the chill of night. The
gardens are almost empty, leaving behind the stringy vine
plants and other remnants. Pumpkins are beginning to
ripen to bright orange. Soon, the families will be passing
through to find the perfect one to carve for Halloween.

Fall has moved in for a while. The dew falls heavy and creates frosty
designs on the windowpanes. As the sun comes up over the treetops,
its warmth begins to melt the icy artwork. Soon the mittens, hats,
and scarves will be taken out of hiding for another winter season.
And so it goes. Winter will turn into Spring, and those
things that have been sleeping will awaken to the sounds
of birds singing, frogs croaking, and the unmistakable
sound of the insect world going about their day.
Nature is busy planning and preparing itself,
yet again. Aren't the seasons glorious!
I want to be kissed by the warmth of the sun and have my hair
mussed by the gentle breezes that blow and keep things moving.
Time does not stand still.

I Feel

When I awake and hear the chirping and whistles of birds, I feel.
When I look in the sky and see shapes in the clouds, I feel.
When I see a bird catching updrafts in flight, I feel.
When the vibrant colour of my garden lily reveals itself, I feel.
When the apple blossoms open and scent the breeze, I feel.
When butterflies effortlessly float from flower to flower, I feel.
When the leafy branches sway in the wind, I feel.
When the sun's reflection sparkles like
diamonds on calm waters, I feel.
When the sounds of children playing fill the air, I feel.
When I see a person smile, I feel.
When I am in the presence of my family, I feel.
When I remember my mother and father, I feel.
When I feel, it reminds me I'm alive and I am grateful.
I'm alive and I recognize it as a gift and I thank You.
I can see, and the beauty fills me with wonder.
I can hear, and the sounds are like music.
I can feel, and my heart is overflowing.

Nature's Gifts

Blue sky, sunshine, rain, snow, and storms
He created the weather in all of its forms.
Beauty can be found in each and every one.
Most favourite types of weather usually involve the sun.
We all have our preference. Mine is blue sky and warm breeze.
Some prefer snow fall, but I don't like to freeze.
They all have their purpose in our day-to-day world.
For plants that were drying out, the rainfall unfurled.
Thunderstorms have a way of refreshing everything.
That's when you will hear the creatures that can sing.
They make a joyful noise. It's their way of giving praise
to the One who is and was and will be, for always.

The Four Seasons

Spring, what an appropriate name for this season.
It means, to show energy and action. Spring does this
rather quickly and with dedicated purpose.

My favourite season is Summer. The perfect day has a gentle
warm breeze, gently blowing through the leaves on the trees
or cooling sun-kissed skin. The sky is that beautiful shade of
blue with a few white clouds drifting overhead. The waterways
glisten like a treasure chest full of diamonds and the sound
of children's excited chatter as they play along the beach.
In the evenings, I sit out on my sunporch and wait for the majesty
of the sunset colours to make my heart skip a beat. I listen to the
sounds of the woods and fields as the wildlife settles for the night.

Autumn is a lovely season, but it makes me sad. This is when
the awe-inspiring array of colour is drained from the landscape.
The leaves, just as they had unfurled to life, now slowly dry
and curl back in death. They die on the branch and break
away to blow in the wind before settling to decompose. Their
new job is giving every last bit of nutrient back to the earth
for a new season and a new life of beauty, but until then …

The trunk of the tree draws all of its moisture into itself. It will
need it to feed and maintain its strength for the harsh season ahead.
The trees are standing tall in their naked frailty as the harsh
winds of Autumn break small branches and even hearty limbs
from them. They continue to stand tall against the onslaught.

The temperature continues to plummet until the rains of Fall turn into sleet and snow and ice. A new season has begun. It is named Winter. This season is a bully. It can be sweet and beautiful in its stark whiteness, blanketing the land in a thick quilt like a freshly made bed. Don't be fooled. It can turn on a dime. You may wake the next morning to such a large snowfall that you are unable to go about your daily routines, until roads are cleared and vehicles are uncovered.

You may awaken to a beautiful, ice sculptured scene that has encapsulated the world outside your window. It is amazing in its glistening and sparkling beauty, but look beyond the beauty and look to the devastation. Trees are destroyed, as they can no longer hold up under the weight of their ice-covered branches and are ripped and violently torn from the trees. Power lines have fallen for the same reason. Homes are without the life-sustaining power needed for the daily grind of life. The roads are death traps for any travellers who are caught unaware, or those who foolishly think they can get to where they need to go.

It tries the human spirit. So when the sun comes out, the sky is blue, and the evergreens are a vibrant contrast between earth and sky, we venture out to find reprieve in the beauty of the day. There are a variety of activities to enjoy, from snowmobiling to ice fishing, to sledding and skiing, to fort-building and making angels in the snow.

The end of winter is finally approaching. It can be seen in higher temperatures, reduced snowfall, melting snow, new growth pushing up through the bare patches of ground, and tiny buds beginning their cycle of life along the tree limbs. The birds sing brightly. The animals come out to enjoy the changes of the seasons. Spring is new life. Natures' wildlife are birthing and hatching babies.

The sounds of Spring are a symphony of music to be enjoyed. The cycle begins again. I love to sit out on my sunporch in the evening and listen, as my reverie is joyfully broken by the chirping of frogs down by the creek or the last warbles of birds settling in their nests for the night.

Among the Clouds

We floated in the heavens
among the landscape of clouds.
I saw all shapes and sizes.
Some enveloped us like shrouds.
I even saw some vertical ones
standing straight and tall.
They looked like giant soldiers
standing guard at the royal wall.
The plane dropped a little lower
and I saw a different scene.
These clouds looked like an Alaskan winter,
all cold, stark, and pristine.
The next scene laid out before me
was a sunset made of red.
It looked like lava, flowing down a hillside
from my position overhead.
I had flown a few times before,
but had never taken the time
to look at the world from this perspective.
It is truly quite sublime.
His miracles are everywhere.
They're on the earth and in the sky.
I get lost in the beauty of it all
and keep them safe in my mind's eye.

The Cycle of Life

The season is changing.
The air has a chill.
We are coming into Autumn
and all the colours that will fill
the leaves of the maple trees.
They'll give everything they've got
before falling to the ground,
where they will stay until they rot.
The earth will use all the nutrients
that the debris has to offer.
Nothing will go to waste,
but will be stored for the winter.
The snow will act as insulation,
keeping the nutrients dormant till Spring,
when the ground will produce good soil
that will feed everything.
It's called the cycle of life.
We live and then we die.
We leave behind a legacy
for our families to live by.
Family is most important
and the best thing we'll ever know.
Let's love them and teach them
and help them to grow.
It's when we teach our children
what's right and what's wrong,
that we can witness them grow into
a loving person who is strong.

Surrender

It is one of those hot, humid days again. The kind where you can't
find any relief. The least bit of movement that your body makes
creates additional sweat to release itself from your skin. There is
a cold clammy layer all over your body that soaks into anything
that it comes into contact with. You have to keep pulling your
shirt away from yourself or change your shirt again altogether.
I wipe the moisture from my face and neck with a tissue. It wads up
as it absorbs and disintegrates in my hand. I throw it out and use
a fresh one to finish the job. I sit close to a fan and get some relief,
but as soon as I move away, my body creates a fresh layer of wet,
clammy moisture and my shirt is sticking again. I can feel the sweat
trickling down the centre of my back. I run my fingers through
my hair and it is, in strings, all stuck together with tiny drops of
water, clinging to the ends and waiting to drip onto my clothes.
These temperatures sap us of our energy and strength. We
don't feel like doing anything, but try to find some sort of
relief from it. I find myself in front of the fan, again …

Blessed

He has a strength about him that makes me smile inside.
He deals with what he has been given and will not run and hide.
He is not afraid to open the door and deal with the devil himself.
God forbid that the devil should speak,
because he'd get a shot in the mouth.
Nothing seems to faze him much. He takes it all in stride.
He's been given the strength of ten thousand
men, because in him, God resides.
He counts his blessings every day and gives praise to the Lord above.
He looks at his pain as gifts from God,
sent with an abundance of love.

What Makes a True Friend?

The qualities that altogether make a true friend are many.
They include love, respect, understanding, laughter, non-judgement, supportiveness, good listening with soft eyes,
similar likes, trustworthiness, honesty, and a confidante.
True friends do not come by the truckload. They can
be few and far between. Some people never meet them.
When you find a treasure, like a true friend, you know
how rare and special that is and you value them.
When someone feels valued, it makes their heart feel the
warmth of the love extended to them. To go through this
life and be rich enough to feel the love of true friendship
can almost make one weep with gratitude. Life becomes
brighter and sweeter. Difficult times are easier to combat,
and successes are more meaningful when shared.
I hope that everyone has an opportunity to find a treasure
like a true friend and recognize them for the gift that they
are and to cherish them sweetly, purely, and lovingly.
Some people find a true friend in a sibling(s), a relative, a spouse,
a co-worker, or a newcomer. If you consider your sibling(s)
as your friend, how lucky are you? If you marry someone
who becomes your true friend, what a blessing, and if you are
someone who has met a co-worker or a newcomer and that
acquaintance turns into a true friend, then what good fortune.
We are put in the path of some people on purpose or by
design. That is a destiny that you were fated for.
True friends are like four leaf clovers. They are worthy of the time
and effort it takes to find one, because they are rarer than you think.
May you wake up every morning with the knowledge
that you are loved and cherished by a kindred spirit.

Mother Friend

The love you give to your newborn child comes of its own accord.
It nurtures and grows as the child does with
the love that you've outpoured.
Time goes by and the seasons change. They're
not always on your favourite list.
But late at night, when you gaze at their
faces, you see what you have missed.
More time goes by faster, it seems, of which you have no control.
They will soon be grown and out on their
own. Wasn't that the goal?
Why do you feel so lonely at times? You know that they're okay.
They seem to miss you as much and try to call you every day.
The next few years can bring many changes, one of them a baby.
You are a grandma now, and she's quite the little lady.
You gaze into those little eyes that are worth
more than their weight in gold.
This is what it's all about. Your love is returned, tenfold.
A mother's job is never done. You will be one forever and ever.
It is a bond that is so strong no one can ever sever.
You are part of a growing legacy and one
that you should be proud of.
Your children have found each other again.
Prayers answered, with the Father's love.

Lovely Soul

We have been friends for almost 12 years
and became kindred shortly after.
We have felt loved and supported
and filled each other with such laughter,
for each other is unique
and can easily stand apart.
But together we are a force.
We love each other's heart.
As you once pointed out, you are my muse.
We share things with each other that are hard to bear alone.
The other makes it bearable.
Thank goodness for the telephone.
For those times when we lived a few provinces apart,
the phone calls were the lifeline in a friendship still tied
by genuine love and care for the other.
You were always there for me, especially when my mom died.
True friends are there, not just for the joys,
the dinner parties, and camping trips.
We rally around whenever we are called.
We help each other get past the falls and slips.
Life becomes richer and has much more substance.
It never matters how long we are apart.
The years go by and we grow and learn.
We will always be kindred and love each other's heart.

To My Love

The fir tree branches are laden with snow,
and the air is crisp and clean.
He looks around and smiles to himself at the
wonders of the beauty he's seen.
His gaze drifts higher and he sends up a prayer
filled with humble thanks and praise.
This is the place God has chosen for him
to spend the rest of his days.
There is a lot to be done. The dreams have
been shared. Excitement is all around.
He sees his dream come to life in his
mind, and he is honour-bound.
He will bring those dreams to reality and
enjoy every step of the way.
For he is a man God blessed with great
faith, and this is his special day.

Love

Love is wonderful, but it can't stand alone.
You need faith and respect and kindness to be shown.
Friendship comes first and then when that grows,
true love will follow and that's how it goes.
It will have its bumps, potholes, and turns,
but that's the thing that everyone learns.
Life is a gift and gifts should be shared.
You took a chance. You loved and you cared.
To know how it feels to be cherished and loved
is the greatest gift from the Father above.
It won't be easy, but worth every strife.
The gift of true love is eternal life.

Reborn

Things had become dire and decisions had to be made.
There was a new medication, a last resort, they said.
Before it could be finalized, your health hit a new low.
The only option left for you was that your liver had to go.
The idea of a transplant was one that gave you fear.
You talked at great length with your family,
as you wiped away a tear.
This forced you to talk about your own mortality.
What it would mean, if you lost your family.
In your heart, you knew that you were fine with however it went.
But when you thought about your family,
that made your heart feel rent.
You prayed with everything in your heart
and asked for Him to guide you.
A tranquil peace fell upon your soul and
you knew what you had to do.
You were added to the transplant list and now only had to wait.
Unfortunately, your health was declining at an alarming rate.
You were rushed to the hospital to have a paracentesis.
You were feeling like you were slowly
dying and breaking into pieces.
You weren't there long, when you were told
that a perfect match was found.
The joy you felt cannot be described. It was
a miracle and quite profound.
The surgery has been performed and was a great success.
If anyone asks if miracles are real, the answer is yes, yes, yes!
Twice, our Lord gave you life. That must tell you something.
He still has work for you to do and knows
you'll proclaim Him King.
When people ask about your God, the wherefore, and the why,
you will stand and praise His works, and to all, testify.

His Love Everlasting

A celebration is coming. We are awaiting the Saviour's birth.
A star shone bright in the sky that night, a
beacon of immeasurable worth.
Some wise men were asked to follow the
star and see what they could see.
Rumour had it that the Child would be
great, so Herod put out a decree.
He was looking for all male babies that
were born on that day, at night.
He told the men that whatever they did, not to lose the star of light.
The wise men knew that what they had seen
was nothing short of a miracle.
They bowed their heads and off they went,
singing praises, oh so lyrical.
As the Boy grew, it became apparent that
He was created for higher things.
He took the years to travel and learn about all that His faith brings.
To faraway places, He would travel to bring God's word of salvation.
He spent those years gathering believers
and preaching to every nation.
It was inevitable, I guess, that the leaders
would have Him condemned
and that His followers would, through their
fear, deny Him to be their friend.
They had Him followed, to see if they
could trap Him with all He said
and try to win back all the crowds of believers that He had led.
They drummed up bogus charges so that
He would be seen by Pilate.
Pilate said it was a waste of his time and that he didn't buy it.
There was nothing that this man had done to warrant incarceration.
The leaders tried to tell the judge that Jesus was in violation.

This man was saying many things, and
these men saw it as scheming.
They said that He was telling lies, and worst of all, blaspheming.
They said He called himself a king. Just who did He think He was?
We have a king and it's not Him, this man they call Jesus.
When asked by Pilate to explain Himself and to get out of this jam.
Jesus simply looked at him and said, "Who do you say I am?"
Pilate went before the crowd and said, "I can find no reason.
This man has broken no law, I see, so I am going to free Him."
The crowd refused to let it go and were not happy with his decision.
He wanted to placate the crowd, so he gave them another option.
He brought before them a hardened criminal
and asked between the two,
"Who do you want to free today? I'll leave it up to you."
They said to free Barabbas. Pilate's expression was turning grim.
He pointed to Jesus and shrugged his shoulders
and the crowd shouted, "Crucify Him."
Pilate knew he had no choice but to give them what they wanted.
The people were yelling and spitting at Jesus,
while others stood and taunted.
He was stripped down and flogged so violently,
with his flesh all ripped and torn.
He was bleeding from every gash and tear
that was given with all their scorn.
Now came the part that had all prisoners carry their own cross.
They were paraded through the town to
show the people who was boss.
The walk was long, the cross was heavy, and
His robe was sticking to bloody flesh.
He was stumbling and taking too long, so they
looked for someone young and fresh.

They spotted a man that was in that crowd
who looked to fit the bill.
They grabbed him and made him help Jesus
carry the cross up the rest of the hill.
When they reached the spot where it would occur,
the man had helped Jesus the best he could.
All he could do now was watch as they nailed
this Man to the cross of wood.
Mary wept at the feet of her Beloved Son as
the weather turned very ominous.
The One that put Him on this earth was
showing Who was Dominus.
He was angry at how we treated His son. We had gone too far.
What will it take for us to see exactly what we are?
We are selfish beings who think only of
ourselves and forget what Jesus said.
He took all of our hate, anger, and wrath,
and died so that we might be fed.
The word of God is the only word that we should be listening to.
No one said it better than Jesus and He said it to me and you.
Life on earth is not going to be easy. Lots of
choices will be put in your way.
He leaves it up to us to decide what we'll do and what we'll say.
Will we be strong and just and true and live the life that's hard,
or will we become weak and lazy and soon, the devil's ward?
If we want easy, then know where it leads.
To the fires of hell, be sure.
Don't let the devil come with his fishing
pole and you be his fishing lure.

New

He was born into a world that was about to meet their King.
He was so tiny and beautiful and a powerful little thing.
His parents didn't fully understand the undertaking of it all,
but their faith was strong and they answered the call.
The Child grew up with love and faith and a wisdom in all things.
His experiences were grooming Him in all that His life brings.
He grew up knowing in His heart the road He had to travel.
He knew that as He listened and learned, the story would unravel.
The main part of this story would begin when He reached thirty.
He talked with people as He walked on the road, so dusty and dirty.
He would start talking to one person and then it would be two.
Before long, the crowds were gathering,
and the numbers grew and grew.
He brought such a peace and calmness
with Him everywhere He went.
They were gathering by the thousands
now, with no shelter from a tent.
They were in the great wide open. Some sat while others stood.
He spoke about the importance of being faithful, kind, and good.
He said to love thy neighbour and to turn the other cheek.
If we can live our lives this way, we can achieve what it is we seek.
Jesus knew what was in store for Him. One
of us would have run away in fear.
But Jesus loved us so very much that His choice was very clear.
He wanted us all to have the chance, to make it into heaven.
So at the last supper, He held up the wine
and the bread that was unleavened.
He said of the bread, "This is My body,
and the wine, this is My blood.
Those of you who partake in Me, must live a life of good.
If this is the path that you should choose, then know this to be true.
You will always live in Me and I will live in you."

117

This Special Day

The day dawned bright with sunshine
and there was a crispness in the air.
A Babe was born to a Virgin named Mary and
her husband Joseph, an obedient pair.
A star shone bright to light the way
for all to come and see.
Rumour said a Saviour was born.
He has come to save you and me.
They came and knelt before Him
with a reverence so full of awe
to be a witness of this Child Saviour,
the most incredible thing they ever saw.
They came with gifts of thanks and praise
and all began to hum.
They were trying to keep rhythm
with the boy who played his drum.
He came to also witness, but had no gift in hand.
He decided to play a song instead
and knelt down in the sand.
He couldn't take his eyes off the sight
of the Babe that was nestled in the hay.
His heart was so full of joy and love
as he wished the Babe happy birthday.
The Infant was named Jesus.
God saves, is the meaning of His name.
So, Merry Christmas to us all
and glory to Him, we will proclaim.

On the Backs of Soldiers

We fought for your freedom and many lives were lost,
but when we fight for freedom, that is the cost.
We drew a line in the sand.
When the enemy crossed it, then war was at hand.
When the bullets were gone, we relied on our fist.
Those that lost the fight laid dead in the mist.
It rained for a time, and then rained some more.
The mud it created soaked us to the core.
It was everywhere we placed our foot.
It even tried to take our boot.
When we had a moment, we would write to our loved ones
that helped us remember we were daughters and sons.
We had parents who loved us and families of our own.
We would do it again, for we were never alone.
We helped build this country from pillar to post,
and that is what makes us proudest the most.

Remember

They were babes in arms and in a strange land.
They were far from home with rifle in hand.
All they had were their comrades in arms.
The enemy was advancing. Sound the alarms!
They were numbered in the thousands and it was dark outside.
The young ones were trying to be brave and not hide.
It took all of their strength to push on from each place.
The lives that were lost all had a face.
They would not be forgotten. They gave all they had.
They fought for our freedom and boy are we glad.
Because of their action, we have all that we have.
Thank you to all who answered the call.
Even in death, you can all stand tall.
Our history is all because of you.
All we can say is thank you, thank you!

Time

I wonder about the things I have to do.
Sometimes I feel overwhelmed and panic a bit too.
Others with the same tasks would probably do them better.
All I can do is try my best and learn to be happy with what I have.
What do I have?
I have a wonderful life partner who loves and appreciates me.
He tries to give me all that I need, and we
are always there for each other.
I have a family I love and depend on for conversation and support.
I have great friends who love me for me.
As I write this, I feel so selfish, for my worry
and the stress I put upon myself.
I am truly thankful for my life.
It is unfolding as it is supposed to, with God at the helm.
He is my Lord and Saviour, and He saves
me every day, by simply loving me.
He never left me, not even for a second.
Each step I take leads directly to His feet. I will gladly
crawl to find His gifts of love, peace, and eternal
life, because it's where my faith leads me.

I'll Try

You made me look inside myself, and one thing became quite clear.
You were right when you said I didn't come
clean and maybe it was fear.
You said it was all in how you look at
things, that perspective is the key.
You can look at life in a positive light or with negativity.
I know the first choice is the right one, but
I got caught up in making excuses.
It didn't do me any good, but just made me feel foolish.
So, after we talked, I made a promise and one I intend to keep.
I need to always be honest and true and not be afraid, to dig deep.
I did feel better after our chat and should
have said so before we said goodbye.
I want to thank you for your friendship, and know I will always try.

Tell Me

Why is it, whenever we chat on the phone, I do all the sharing?
Is it because you have nothing to say, or am I overbearing?
I thought our friendship was based on trust. Tell me if you agree.
Is our friendship as special to you as it is to me?
There are times when I get off the phone with
you and I feel like you're holding back.
I can't help wondering why you won't confide.
Is there something that I lack?
Why won't you give me the chance to prove
that you can trust me with anything.
I will treat you with the utmost care and all the love I can bring.
I promise it will get easier with every secret you share.
Don't ever feel afraid to tell me. I will always be there.

Senses

To touch.
To smell.
To taste, hear, and see.
These are gifts that allow us to be.
Texture.
Odour.
Flavour, sound, and sight.
These helps us to live with all of our might.
Soft.
Floral.
Sweet, melodious, and inspiring.
Of this incredible life, there will be no tiring
with so much to do and so little time to do it.
Live life to the fullest and make sure God is in it.

Scent Memories

Why is it that certain odours trigger our memories and can throw us right back to the moment that they first impacted us? I stepped out onto the sun porch and was pleasantly assaulted by a most beautiful floral scent. I caught myself inhaling a few more times just to set the smell in my mind. It made me smile when I realized I was checking my mind files for a happy reflection of the past. I have drunk in this particular perfume so many times that there is no "one time" that I can put my finger on. It is a mixture of wild blossom and sweet sap, and it drifts on the breeze as the wind blows.

Filled

I feel so blessed in my life so far.
I love many and am loved as well.
I cherish the love that is sent my way.
It is abundant where I dwell.

My blessings come in all sizes and forms
of people, feelings, and graces.
I try to earn the love I'm given.
It can be found in many places.

I find it in the warmth of an embrace,
a smile, a laugh, or a touch.
We all need blessings in our lives.
We need them very much.

Blessings are appreciated and looked for every day.
We look for them when times are hard.
They can change the way we feel,
like very heartfelt words that are whispered in a card.

When you search for the perfect verse,
you may read piece after piece.
When you come upon the one that's right,
will wonders never cease?

You snatch it up before someone else takes it.
You read it all the way to the till.
The smile on your face is noticed by others.
You hope your smile will catch on and it will.

This is the Season of miracles.
They happen around us every day.
If you need a blessing or a miracle,
all you have to do is pray.

It Matters!

Why do we look into the past?
We can't change anything about it.
We need to keep looking straight ahead
to see where it is that we fit.
We fit in all of our experiences.
It's all about our own perspective.
However we choose to handle it
will impact how we choose to live.
If we always put our best foot forward
and are careful how we place our feet.
When we look at how far we have come,
our past will never show defeat.
Defeat sounds more like giving up.
Instead, look at the past as mapping.
It will lead you in many directions.
So don't you get caught napping.
Your eyes must stay wide open.
Then you will see all your choices.
This is where it will get tough.
Don't get distracted by all the noises.
Keep your eye on the prize of life.
To get there will take all of your wits.
What you will find when you get there
is that everything you did all fits.

In the Silence

Prayer is a gift.
Love is a choice.
Peace is a wish.

What I Know

Time is measured in seconds, minutes, and hours.
Weather is measured in snow, sunshine, and showers.
But love is yours, mine, and ours.

Drift or Swim

Why do I allow my heart to drift away from Yours?
Why do I go through my days closing opened doors?
Sometimes I find it very hard to live as You ask me to.
It doesn't take as much of an effort to do what I want to do.
Happiness doesn't always come and my conscience calls my name.
I ignore the voice that will tell me the truth,
because what I feel is shame.
I tuck it away and do something else to
take my mind off of my action.
If I wait long enough, maybe my mind will ease up a little fraction.
I look in the mirror and see my reflection.
Something has changed in me.
I notice that I don't make eye contact. I look, but I can't see.
What I thought would bring me happiness did nothing of the kind.
All it did was confuse me when I looked inside my mind.
I asked myself the question, what did I want out of this life?
I wanted faith, love, and mercy, and I knew there would be strife.
I was willing to work hard for my family and for myself.
This would involve reading the word of
God, so I took it off the shelf.
I have noticed a deepening of my faith and look at each new day.
I know now which path to take.
Following Jesus is the way.

The Agony in Your Garden

Just as Jesus was tempted by Satan, He has
given you a glimpse of His trials
to show you just how strong you are and how many are the miles.
You have walked quite a way with the help of your
God, and He says, "You're not done yet."
Even if it may seem that you're out on the sea, fishing without a net.
Although your struggles are filled with pain
and you can't always see the end,
He gave you all the strength you'll need. Your tree still has to bend.
At times, it will seem that your tree will break
and it has bent as much as it can handle.
Think of yourself as a flame in the wind,
attached to an endless candle.
No matter how much pain you endure, your light will never dim.
He is very much in you and you're very much in Him.
Your agony is your gift to Him. You will do whatever you need.
In the garden that He gave to you, you are its only seed.

Siblings

Brothers and sisters are one of the best gifts from God.
We rely on each other like peas in a pod.
We are ears of understanding with love and support.
We are there in all situations of every kind and sort.
We laugh the loudest and think the other is funny.
We're the light in the sky when it isn't very sunny.
We are so very different and yet we're the same.
We love each other fiercely, but then that is our aim.
We come together when able and bathe in the light.
We will love each other forever with all of our might.

Childhood

The past comes racing to the forefront of my mind. I was walking in the field when the scent of damp earth, lilac, and wild blossoms sent me back to the spring of 1974. My little sisters and I were looking for wildflowers to pick for our mother one Saturday morning. Our search took us down to the creek, and we looked for frogs and minnows instead. There was an odd-shaped trunk of a tree that kind of reminded us of a horse's back. It was long enough that all four of us could sit on it and ride on our imagination, anywhere we wanted to go. Galloping in a wide-open space was a favourite of mine, because then I could go fast and have the wind whipping at my hair as I commanded the horse to jump over a cedar fence. We all climbed down, and our attention was quickly taken by a snake, slithering along the bank. It must have been looking for lunch, which reminded me that I was getting a bit peckish myself. I asked my sisters if they were getting hungry, to which they all chimed yes! We made our way back to the house for sustenance so that we could continue our adventure after lunch.

Life

We are born into this world new.
We are loved, fed, and cared for.
We are taught and we learn.
Our parents watch us to see how we do.
We are loved, fed, and cared for.
We are taught and we learn.
Our parents make sure our mistakes are few.
We are loved, fed, and cared for.
We are taught and we learn.
We are growing up and learning what to do.
We are loved, fed, and cared for.
We are taught and learn.
We are making decisions on where, what, and who.
We are always loved, but now care for ourselves.
We teach and we learn.
Our parents are proud of how well we grew.
We are loved and now care for others.
We teach and we learn.
We look back and think how fast time flew.
We are loved and are cared for.
We are taught and we learn.
When I am gone, remember, faith was the glue.

Father's Day

What is a Father?
A father is half of the love that made you.
He is your protector, provider, guide, teacher, and
doctor of cuts, scrapes, and general booboos.
He is the ultimate fixer of all broken toys.
He is the tuner of guitars.
He is the rodent killer to calm the screams.
He is the practical joker who loves to spread laughter.
He is the designated driver for all school-sporting events.
He comes in the room on a stormy night to close all windows.
He is the maker of hot cereal to give us all a great start to our day.
His are the arms we run to when life is a struggle.
His is the arm we want to walk us down the aisle.
He is our Patriarch.
He is our Father.
Thank you for giving us the example of
living a good and honest life.
We love you very much, Dad.
Happy Father's Day, today and always.

Celebrate

She was on this earth for 85 years and
accomplished a great many things.
She met and married the man God chose,
and there began her dreams.
Together, they had nine girls and one boy
and raised us with love and respect.
They were always a united front. Their discipline had great effect.
She taught us all, to cook and bake and help her in the kitchen.
She taught us when we were invited out to ask if we could pitch in.
She was proud of us all for the paths that we
took and how we treated others.
We lost her some years ago. She was the Mother of all Mothers.
I hope that when I reach her age, I will have the grace that she had.
I am happy with the time that God gave
her to us, and I will never be sad.

Our Mother

On the three-year anniversary of our Mother's incredible journey, I am struck by how much time has passed and the contradiction in my mind of it all. I say, "How can she have been gone for that length of time already?" But it has been that long. I talked with a dear friend of hers the other day, and she shared how very much she misses her too. The times they shared were many, and at the same time, too few. My heart swells, almost painfully, with pride at the indelible mark our mother left. She was so blissfully unaware of how she touched the hearts, souls, and minds of the people she met along the way. Her life was a testament to her Father. She lived each day, trying to be good, honest, merciful, and loving. She knew she had some shortcomings, as we all do, but that made her all the more earnest and stalwart in her daily life. She taught us to always live our life with God first and everyone and everything else, second. I think God always smiled when he thought of her, looked at her, and especially when he got to bring her home. Thank you, God, for looking after her so very well and for so very long. She was your gift to us all, and one that was so very special. She was Your good and faithful servant to the very end. I love you, Mom.

The Patriarch

The head of the clan is old and frail now. He moves so slowly and carefully, so as not to stumble or fall. He is the last of his siblings and looked upon as the father figure to all his nieces and nephews. Just the knowledge that he is there is a comfort. He travels from place to place with his walker now. It acts as a pair of strong arms to give him the balance he requires to maneuver from room to room. His vibrant ways have been reduced to cards, conversation, and lots of laughter. He is the one now that all of his children call to check in with. They share personal anecdotes that add a smile, even a chuckle to the phone call, or chat across the kitchen table while playing a game of cards. He looks at the life he chose and an expression of pride settles in his eyes. He thinks of his ten children with pride and is now in a position to help whenever needed. This fills him with joy as he is now able to help his children in many more ways. He knows Mom is happy with all of his decisions. She continues to fill his heart with love and comfort.

How

How can it be that you've been gone for so long?
It's frightening how fast the time has flown.
I think about you every day. I love and miss you in every way.
I miss our long conversations on the telephone.
I miss your giggle. You know the one.
You always found the recipe that I asked for.
You hugged me a little longer when you knew I needed more.
Whenever I had a question, you were my sounding board.
You had so much to teach me and I hung on your every word.
I hope when you see me now, I make you proud.
I will always hear you in my heart.
The sound is joyous and loud.

Christmas Dinner with Our Family

The soft yellow glow seeped through the window coverings.
Laughter and joy could be heard all the way to the end of the drive.
This was a house where love lived. It had been nurtured by the
parents of this clan. The mother had passed a few years before,
and the father was alone, the light of their family. They gave
a toast for their mother at every gathering and had incredible
family time together. There were drinks and stories, followed
by a joyous feast prepared by the hosts and enjoyed by all.
All through the meal, the memories flowed. You could almost
reach out and physically touch the love that accompanied
it all. As the main course was finished, orders were being
taken for dessert. There was always a lot, so seconds were
offered. Some had room for one more small piece. Of course,
there was always room for the topping as well. Will that be
whipped cream or ice cream? The usual answer was yes!
When the plates were cleared and coffee was served, whoever
was able to get mobile generally started dishes. The moans
and groans could be heard from the kitchen as someone
made an attempt to stand and find refuge on a couch.
We invariably congregate in the games room, where a game of
pool had challenger's names being added to the chalkboard.
There was a never-ending stream of game critique and more laughs
as someone was probably getting annihilated. That's okay, the next
person was already standing at the ready with pool cue in hand.
The lovely evening ended with lots of thanks and hugs
and kisses, because that always speaks from the heart.
Bye for now, until the next celebration.

Family Times

Shining lights, laughter, giggles, hugs, and kisses.
The heart grows with the love of family.
Small groups are gathered all over the house.
Nestled in close conversation.
It is months between visits, and there is
always a lot to get caught up on.
Enticing smells permeate the home.
The clinking of glasses can be heard among the murmurs.
Everyone is called to come and share the Christmas feast.
We bow our heads and give thanks for the
food and the family to share it with.
The desserts are many, so someone takes the orders.
We push ourselves away from the table to begin cleanup.
You can hear the conversations start up again.
Some will retire to the game room to try and
work off the effects of the meal.
Some move to the kitchen to put away leftovers
and others fill the sink with hot soapy water to
wash the pots and more delicate items
that never see the dishwasher.
It is the time for the first ones to pack up
and prepare for the long trek home.
Others try to squeeze as much time out
of the celebration as possible.
Soon, the last of the visitors have loaded
their vehicles and headed home.
Another joyous gathering had by all.
May each and every one have a Merry Christmas
and the Happiest of New Years.

Thank You, Ireland

She was born on the Emerald Isle,
the most beautiful shades of green.
Mother looked into the eyes of child
and felt a love that had always been.
They shared a very special bond.
The love was incredibly deep.
Even when they were apart,
in touch they would always keep.
The daughter moved to another country.
She got married and had a family of her own.
This woman is faithful, gentle, and kind,
and her children are all grown.
This woman herself is a giver of things.
She gives her faith, her time, her care, and her love.
She is loved in return, more than she knows,
especially from her Father above.

Her Marathon of Life

Fran won her race all those years ago.
Her Father said, "On your mark, get set, go!"
She ran all the way to the pearly gate.
Where she thought she would have to wait,
St. Peter said, "Great job! Well done!
Come on in and meet Your Father's Son."
Fran walked right into His embrace.
He kissed her and congratulated her on her race.

Christmas Joy

Their bright shining eyes are wide with anticipation.
The house has been adorned with lights, all in preparation.
Christmas Eve will soon be here and Midnight Mass attended.
When all return to the house that night, a gift will be presented.
The special little presents are unwrapped before the fire.
New ornaments for next year and then we all retire.
The little ones are tucked in tight, with a kiss upon their head.
Later that night, when they're asleep, a filled
stocking is placed on the bed.
The morning light finds its way through the
curtains and children begin to rise.
They sit up in bed and look at the stocking
that's filled with a little surprise.
The smell of their favourite Christmas breakfast
has them running to the table.
Pancakes with bacon or sausage and orange
juice is enjoyed by all who are able.
After everyone has had their fill, they gather round the tree.
Presents are opened and smiles are shared.
All are as happy as can be.
Mom goes to the kitchen to make the stuffing for the turkey.
The pies are baking in the oven. She made
pumpkin, apple, and blueberry.
The pies come out and the turkey goes in. It will be ready on time.
The children get dressed and play out in the
snow, while the adults enjoy some wine.
The meal was enjoyed and the dishes are
done. It has been a rather long day.
To our Lord Jesus, I would like to wish a very Happy Birthday!

Dad

I hope that when you are sitting in the silence, you can hear
the murmurs of prayer and love that we feel for you.
I hope that when you bow your head in
prayer, you feel us praying with you.
I hope that when you close your eyes, your dreams are
filled with the life you shared with Mom and all of us.
I hope your memories catch you by surprise when
they make you smile and laugh out loud.
I hope that when you sleep, you feel His arms
holding you lovingly through the night.
I hope you are proud of the job you did
on helping to raise us in faith.
I know you are prepared for the day that He will call you.
I know He is pleased with His good and faithful servant.
You have lived your whole life with Him in the driver's seat.
You knew you would be safe in His care.
And here you are, patiently waiting to hear the sound
of your name whispered on the wind just for you
to hear. He will say, "Come home, John."
And you will say, "Here I am, Lord!"

Your Dwelling Place

In your new home, may you always find love.
May your walls echo with hope and faith.
As you grow together in this house,
may you always fill its space
with laughter, mercy, peace, joy,
and everything in between.
My wish for you all is that this home
sees you the happiest that you've ever been.

The Sunflower for Jen

Her spirit loves you and keeps a watchful eye.
She held you when you began to cry.
She stayed with you when you felt despair.
She took up residence in the corner chair.
She knew we loved you, our newfound sis.
And she comforted you with a gentle kiss.
She missed out on knowing you all those years ago.
She knows you now and loves you so. From
her kitchen, I give you this flower.
It comes with lots of love.
When she sees them hanging in our homes,
know she is smiling from above.

Do you Know

Do you know what you have done for your girls and for your son?
You have fulfilled your promise to God and raised us all as one.
You were both always united in the decisions that you made.
Together, you were a force, and your children always obeyed.
The boundaries were clear and the lines were drawn. We
were taught the right side was the one to be on.
With that side came truth, responsibility,
pride, faith, and personal integrity.
Do you know what you have done?
You taught us that kindness, love, and mercy,
are the soul's favourite food.
And if you live life with these gifts, then life will be quite good.
You have taught us death is a part of life
and you live that truth each day.
You showed us through your strength that living on is the only way.
Our loved ones will leave us, but not by their choice.
They could not say no to the Father's voice.
When your time has come and he whispers in your
ear, His is the voice you've always wanted to hear.
His arms will be open and His eyes will be bright.
He can't wait to hold you for you are His light.

Quiet Kindness

"Do you need some help?" she asked.
I'd reply, "Why yes, if you don't mind."
She always knows just what to say.
She is thoughtful, sweet, and kind.
She puts others first before herself.
Family and friends are most important.
She nurtures those that she loves the most.
Her kindness is her fortune.
She spreads this gift all around.
If you are in need, it is yours.
Take what you need and pass it on.
Watch how your kindness soars.
When you have, then you must share.
Pay it forward and see where it goes.
Bit by bit and drop by drop,
that's how the river flows.
So thank you, my dear. I cherish you.
I hope you know that to be true.
I love it when you come for a visit,
because I love spending time with you.

One Day

Our life plays out before us each day.
Our actions and reactions happen as they may.
We go about our daily chores
like running errands and mopping floors.
We never expect our routine to change.
Our goals are usually within range
then one day starts like all the rest.
There is nothing to prepare us for the mess.
You're unconscious and don't remember much,
and when you come to, you hurt so much.
You hear murmurs from people gathered around you.
You are trying to figure out what you are supposed to do.
You fade in and out, as the pain is too great.
You find peace in oblivion and are unaware of your fate.
There is a commotion out in the hall.
You recognize the voice and this woman so tall.
She has a look of love and fear and calm.
She rushes to your side and kisses your palm.
Just to look at her face and see the joy in her eyes
Is all that you needed to make you realize
how lucky you are to have the ones that you love.
They were given as a gift from your Father above,
so rest in this knowledge as you heal from the pain.
You are so very loved, and that love will sustain.

For You

From nothingness you were created,
and with guidance became a man.
Along the way, you had a family,
and for them, do all you can.
You are respected in your field of work
and in the community that you live.
You are always ready to lend a hand
and offer whatever you can give.
You just celebrated another birthday.
You are now fifty-one years old.
Enjoy all your very special days
and watch how your life unfolds.

The Key

They were together longer than they were apart,
raising children, working hard, and trying to pay the bills.
Their trust in God always got them through the worst part.
Together, they could make it over all the hills.

He was the last-born child in a brood of thirteen.
She was the fourth child born of six.
He was the cutest little boy they'd ever seen.
She was the most shy of her family's mix.

They each went to a young people's dance one night.
He caught a glimpse of her from across the crowded floor.
He couldn't take his eyes from her sight.
He told his friend to look at the vision that
had just walked through the door.

He said to his friend, "That's the girl I'm gonna marry."
She was oblivious to him, as yet.
He approached her and asked her to dance.
And now, she was forever caught in his net.

They married six months later and raised a family of ten.
He could make her laugh till her eyes filled with tears.
Conversations went. "Do you remember when?"
They were married for almost fifty-nine years.

She was the first to leave us in her eighty-sixth year.
He missed her every single day.
In the early years, her memory made him tear.
As time went on, he would bow his head and pray.
He knows God has the plan.
He prayed for patience, mercy, and love.
He was a loving and God-fearing man
and is now with the Father above.

They are now together for eternity.
They will continue to watch over us from above.
They hold on tight to the family key.
They turned it and locked in all their love.

Your Road

I have so much to say to you.
I don't want to miss the opportunity.
The days go by so quickly,
and soon, you will be on your journey.
You walked your road of life,
and it led you straight to her.
You fell in love quite instantly.
She was the one. You knew it for sure.
You shared a life for almost fifty-nine years.
The memories are all you have left of her now.
You are counting the days till you see her again.
It is the promise that was given when you made the vow.
He always keeps His word.
Lies can't live in the light.
You lived your life with love and faith
and prayed with all your might
that God continues to watch over your children
when you have left this life.
"Don't worry!" He said, in answer to your prayers.
"I will always keep them safe."

Your Special Day

Another year has come and gone to mark the day of your birth.
Look in the mirror and see God's love. It glows with all its worth.
His light shines bright within your soul.
You're a witness for all to see,
a witness to His great design. You were given this gift for free.
You live your life from day to day, healing people's blindness.
You help them to see beyond themselves
by showing simple kindness.
Your smile and gentle words are soothing in themselves,
but pair that with your personality and that's when everything gels.
His masterful creations are wonders to behold.
You are exactly one of those, and then He broke the mould.
There is only one, beautiful you. Take flight like the sparrow.
Live the gift of life He gave like there'll never be a tomorrow.

The Gentle Giant

They call him a gentle giant
for his size and for his heart.
He looks as tough as a cement wall
but is as sweet as a butter tart.
Please watch over him, Lord.
Keep him safe and warm.
Guide the surgeon's expert hands.
Protect him from all harm.
We ask this Lord on his behalf.
He needs You by his side.
The doctors have a hard job to do.
They need You as their guide.
You are the One true Healer.
You created all living things.
We ask for blessings on Your child, that
he may reap all that Your healing brings.

Hello Little One

They waited with bated breath
as the surgeon prepared to start.
They had waited for nine long months.
They had heard the beating of his heart.
Dad was feeling overwhelmed,
so he bowed his head to pray.
"God, please keep them both safe
and let me love them for always."
God's love surrounded them with His warmth.
The operating room became quite still.
The gloved hands reached in and cradled the babe.
Holding new life never lost its thrill.
He laid the newborn on mother's chest.
Mother and baby both let out a sigh.
The parents looked at their newborn babe
and both began to cry.
There was no sadness in this room.
All the tears were made of joy.
Their hearts felt like they were going to burst.
Thank you, Lord, for our new baby boy.

Hannah

She has soft brown curls and sun-kissed skin.
When she tells you a joke, you can't help but grin.
She has dancing eyes and a heart of gold.
She seems so wise, but she's not very old.
She always has a smile ready to share.
She treats her loved ones with special care.
She is honest and true and one of a kind.
No better friend would you ever find.
So please take heart. Nasty words don't matter.
They are hurtful, untrue, and were never meant to flatter.
God made you special, so don't ever forget.
You're one of the sweetest girls I've ever met.

Eternity

He wanders through each room and she is there.
Her laughter. Her tears. Her disappointments,
and sometimes, her anger and frustrations.
But it is the faith, joy, and laughter that sing out the loudest,
because there was always way more of that than anything else.
He can see her at the puzzle table with the tip of
her tongue sticking out between her teeth, as she
contemplates where to put the next piece.
He sees her sitting in her recliner, engrossed in a book. He sees her
lay her head back in the chair, close her eyes, and rest for a while.
He sees her scurrying around the kitchen, preparing
a luncheon for their weekly card party.
His favourite place is out on the sunporch, looking at the beautiful
Fall splash of colour. That's when he spots the wild turkeys.
"Fran, come here and see this. They're back!"
He smiles to himself. He forgot for a moment that he will
have to look for the both of them, as she is waiting for him in
another beautiful place, one that he longs to go to one day.
He will tell her all about it then.

The House on the Hill

When I sit down, I dream a dream that
takes me back to the country.
There on the hill sits my childhood home
that's older than a century.
My father dwells in the house alone these last ten months or so.
My family's dream is to buy the house when we're back in Ontario.
The memories of my childhood home
are worth their weight in gold.
My family's dream is to live in this house until we're very old.
We'll sit on the sunporch and watch the sun
setting to the glorious colour of red.
And when we're done, we'll toast the night
and dream our dreams in bed.

Four Walls

The place I grew up in had lots of love, discipline,
sibling rivalry, spats, laughter, jokes, and tears,
as well as a great deal of determination.
It wasn't just a house.
The place I grew up in had expectations, goals
for the future, and pride in one's self.
It wasn't just a house.
The place was full at all times. Full of people. Two
parents, ten children. Full of noise. Twelve voices.
Twelve sets of footsteps. Doors being opened and closed.
Food being prepared and dishes being done.
It wasn't just a house.
The place got less noisy and crowded each year, it seemed.
Someone was leaving for college or an out-of-town job. Some
were getting married and starting their own families.
It wasn't just a house.
We have all grown up and moved away to raise our own families.
There is lots of love, discipline, sibling rivalry, spats,
laughter, jokes, tears, and just as much determination.
We come together in our parent's place whenever we are able.
It's home!

She

She is warmth,
Is loving,
Is kindness,
Is laughter,
Is light.

She was faith filled,
Was gracious,
Was generous,
Was giving,
Was an incredible teacher.

She will always love us,
Will always be loved,
Will always be missed,
Will always pray for us,
Will always be our mother.
She.

Summer Party

She looked down through the misty white clouds. She
couldn't help but be filled with pride and joy at what God,
her husband, and she had created all those years ago.
She felt everything they were feeling. She felt the warmth of their
embraces as they hugged each other and she felt the love they all
have for each other. She felt the joy from all the laughter filling
the air. She smiled at how much her grandchildren and great-
grandchildren had grown. She watched the hustle and bustle of
food being prepared. She loved to see all the different conversations
being shared, each playing catchup since the last get-together.
She saw her children all gathered around their Dad,
loving him and sharing stories with him.
She bowed her head and said a prayer of thanks and
gratitude, for her loved ones and the incredible effort that
they continue to make, to get together, stay together, play
together, and continue this legacy of love. Her heart is full.

Her Journey to Peace

She lay so small alone in her bed,
I crawled in beside her and cradled her head.
I whispered in her ear that I loved her so,
And I told her that it was all right to go.
I held on tight as she drew her last breath.
Her gift from God was a peaceful death.
Her children surrounded her with prayers of peace.
Their love for her will never cease.
I will miss her hug, her laugh, and her smile.
I won't miss them forever, but just for a while.
I know that one day, I will see her again.
She will be healthy and happy and free from the pain.
So I thank You, Lord Jesus, for Your faith, love, and mercy,
but especially for giving her as a mother to me.

Happy Anniversary, Jen

We are gathered around you with our hearts on our sleeve.
You are as strong as can be. It's hard to believe
that one year ago today, we were praying for success.
We were overwhelmed with emotions, but trying our best
to show you our strength, because that's what you needed
to help you through the healing and grow the garden you seeded.
You planted love, hope, and faith, and prayed for good weather
so the garden could grow and we could harvest it together.
You have so much to give, to teach, and to share.
Your wonderful life is our answered prayer.

It's in the Eyes

The tell of a wonderful human being is in the print they leave behind. They are noticed for the way they carry themselves. They appear to have a relaxed easy confidence and self-awareness. When they speak, interesting things always seem to spill from their lips. They take time for anyone who asks for it or needs it. Their heart overflows with kindness. This is the draw. It is like a magnet. The pull happens almost without the person's knowledge of why they feel this person is so approachable and understanding. They are greeted with eye contact and the most beautiful and welcoming smile.

My Prison Heart

I hang on tight to the ones I love.
I keep them in my heart.
I turn the key to set the lock
so it can't be pulled apart.
I'll keep them safe for a lifetime.
After all, that's what true love is.
They say it's unconditional
and sealed with a hug and a kiss.
He fills my heart with His mercy and love.
The ones I love will never be without.
They will sit in the company of God
and discover what their relationship is all about.
Take the time to get to know Him
or deepen the love that's already there.
He looks at you with nothing but love.
The loss of any child, He cannot bear.
So come to Him with open arms
and get wrapped in His embrace.
He will hold you for a lifetime
and gift you with His grace.

Love can conquer all

When you swear a covenant with your love
who was handpicked by God,
that doesn't mean it will be easy
or the road won't be dark.
There is nothing worthwhile about easy.
You have to work hard to make it last.
If you are not prepared to stick with it,
then leave it in the past.
The tears, though full of pain,
are all part of a greater plan.
If you cherish what you have,
all doubt will wash away with the rain.
He will always walk beside you both.
No need to feel afraid.
He did handpick you for each other.
It was the best decision that you ever made.

Miracle

I know a miracle. She has a name.
It is faithful servant of the Lamb that was slain.
He was brutalized by the ignorance of humanity.
It was His gift to us despite our vanity.
She was given the gift of life.
This also became her cross.
She will carry it every day and night
in gratitude for the life that was lost.
This miracle I know is truly like no other.
You see, this gift that she was given
came directly from her Father.
The relationship she has with Him
she cherishes like a precious gem.
She knows Him very intimately.
He is the Great I Am.

Thank You

When I wake up in the morning, I look upon the day.
I thank God I have awakened, and in my prayer, I say,
"Thank you for my blessings and thank You for my health.
You give us all so much. Your gifts are truly wealth.
Help us to recognize the talents You bestowed.
They come with the grace and mercy that You have always showed.
The beauty You chose to surround us with
is breathtaking, to say the least.
Let us look upon it with our eyes and be thankful for the feast.
Always help us to be thankful for everything we've been given.
Let us always share our gifts with those that are still living.
When our time has come, and You choose to call us home.
Give us the gift of understanding to know that Thy will be done."

A Grateful Companion

His excitement showed in his bouncing step.
Maybe today will be the day.
If he is well behaved and calm,
this couple may take him home today.
They put on a leash and brought him outside.
They walked him around the yard.
They gave him a command of sit and stay,
and then a biscuit for a reward.
He had a look in his eyes of love and peace.
He was hopeful of a new home.
The man asked, "Can I choose the name for him?"
All this new property was his to roam.
He lived a good long life with his family.
He loved them very much.
He loved the walks and food and love,
but most of all, their touch.
Thank you for everything you did for me.
You gave me a wonderful life.
I want to take this time to say thank you
to you and to your wife.
You gave me everything I could ever need.
The bed you built for me was awesome.
Don't feel sad for me at all,
because I have your Dad,
and he has his furry grandson.

Ripley

When we first got you, you could fit in the palm of our hand.
You were so small and cute and looking for affection.
There were times that I was afraid I might step on you.
You were my little guy and you needed my protection.
It wasn't long before we had you on a routine.
Feedings, walks, playtime, and naps.
You needed so much attention.
You were dressed in warm coats with matching caps.
I can't believe that soon you'll be thirteen.
The time just seemed to fly right by.
The vet diagnosed you with cancer,
and all I wanted to do, was cry.
I hope you have always felt loved
You were part of our family, you know.
So please, know you will be sorely missed
when it is your time to go.

Kayla

You gave her love, kindness, exercise, and food.
In return, she gave you unconditional love and was good.
She didn't ask for much, as you gave her all she could ask for.
She did her best to keep you safe as she guarded your front door.
Kayla's guarding days are done. She worked right up to the end.
She had to say goodbye to you, but knows your hearts will mend.
She knows you still have love to give and
might get another pet one day.
Don't worry about anything. It will all work out okay.

About the Author

Mary-Ellen was born in Toronto, Ontario, Canada. She lived in Richmond Hill until she was five years old. Her family then moved to a farm in Muskoka, where she completed her elementary and high school education. She moved to Kingston as a live-in nanny for four years, at which time she enrolled at St. Lawrence College in the Child and Youth Counsellor program. She graduated with an award and worked with at risk youth and finished off her career working with special needs children in a school setting. She found her career very rewarding.

She now lives with her husband on the old family homestead. They have a son who is grown, but lives nearby. She has eight sisters and one brother, and all are very close. They get together as often as they can.

She lost her mother in 2011 and her father in 2017. They lived wonderful lives and raised their children in faith. Her mother taught all of her children to cook and bake and that is one of Mary-Ellen's favourite pastimes. She also loves to sing, read, go for walks, and most of all, write. Her sunporch is a favourite setting for the inspiration she gets from looking out at God's incredibly beautiful creation.

CPSIA information can be obtained
at www.ICGtesting.com
Printed in the USA
LVHW03s2344310718
585567LV00001B/36/P